The Vintage Musical Comedy Book

John Drinkrow

The Vintage Musical Comedy Book

Illustrated from the Raymond Mander
and Joe Mitchenson Theatre Collection

 OSPREY

First published in 1974 by
Osprey Publishing Limited
707 Oxford Road, Reading, Berkshire
© Copyright 1974 John Drinkrow
ISBN 0 85045 103 5

Printed in England by
The Camelot Press Ltd, London and Southampton

Contents

8

Illustrations

Introduction

This book is intended to complement my own work, *The Vintage Operetta Book*, and Michael Hardwick's *Osprey Guide to Gilbert and Sullivan* in providing a concise guide to light musical works for the stage which have survived in performance or memory or repute. *The Vintage Operetta Book* dealt with some fifty examples from France, Germany and Austria; this present volume considers ones which originated in England or the United States of America.

There are over seventy of these, and there could, of course, have been more. The permissible size of the volume for its price has been a useful limiting factor in approaching a vast subject. It was not hard to decide where to begin: the production of *Dorothy* in 1886 which marked the beginning of George Edwardes's reign at the Gaiety and then Daly's, in London. Where to drop the curtain was a more difficult question, which I hope I have settled satisfactorily by choosing 1960, the year in which Oscar Hammerstein II's long and distinguished career was ended by his death; though it is with regret that I omit such later successes as *Hello Dolly* and *Oliver*.

It might be argued that 1960 is a trifle late for works to be labelled 'vintage'. Indeed, it seems no time at all since one saw the original runs of some of those included here. Yet, in 1973, it is fifteen years since *My Fair Lady* opened in London, and the first New York audiences had seen it two years before that. In any case, the term 'vintage' implies quality, not age, and who would deny the title to even the most recent work in this book, *The Sound of Music*?

Some readers will find works omitted which they themselves might have chosen for inclusion, and others included which they would have left out. I have tried to be representative of countries, composers and types of work, and have once more based my selection very much upon the advice of Miss Leila S. Mackinlay, the well-known authority on light opera, for which I am deeply grateful. Incidentally, I use the term 'light opera' in no specific sense. At what point – if, indeed, there is one – light opera gives way to musical comedy, the musical play, the play with music, or just the 'musical', I do not know, and don't believe it matters. The term by which I have labelled each work included here is that taken from the score, and presumably given to it by those who created it. The omission of *Porgy and Bess* and *West Side Story* is intentional: the former is certainly opera and the latter, with its grimly realistic theme, is more opera than 'musical', in my view.

Once more I am grateful to Mr Frank Rogers for compiling the Discography, which carries its own introductory note; to the National Operatic and Dramatic Association for making source material available; and to Raymond Mander and Joe Mitchenson for selecting some delightful illustrations from their famous collection.

The Musical Comedies

Annie Get Your Gun, *a musical play in two acts. Music and lyrics by Irving Berlin, book by Herbert and Dorothy Fields. First produced: New York, 1946; London, 1947. Set in America towards the end of the 19th century.* (Performing rights: Emile Littler Musical Plays.)

The star attraction of Buffalo Bill's Wild West Show is Frank Butler, a big, gentle fellow, but a crack shot with a rifle. When the show arrives in Cincinnati its manager, Charlie Davenport, offers 100 dollars to any local who can out-shoot Frank. The challenge is taken up by a noisy, unsophisticated girl, Annie Oakley, who out-guns Frank impressively, but falls in love with him. She has felt the stirrings of love before, though men tend to shy away from her (in her own words, 'You can't get a man with a gun'). While Frank appreciates her abilities, he, too, does not see her as the helplessly feminine type that is his ideal.

Buffalo Bill signs up Annie for the show. Hearing that the rival company, run by Pawnee Bill, has engaged none less than Chief Sitting Bull, Charlie and Buffalo Bill have to devise something spectacular that will draw the publicity their way again. They think up a shooting act on a motor-cycle, which Annie carries off brilliantly. But Frank's pride is hurt as he hears the audience's wild applause and knows that the rival showmen are watching from out in front. He leaves Buffalo Bill and joins the others.

A European tour proves financially disastrous for Buffalo Bill's company and a merger with Pawnee Bill's is proposed and agreed. The question is, how can their respective shooting-stars co-exist? Charlie solves it by disarranging the sights on Annie's gun, so that in a contest

15

with Frank she gets beaten. Frank's pride is assuaged, and Annie gets her man with her defective gun.

PRINCIPAL NUMBERS

Act 1   'Colonel Buffalo Bill' (Charlie and ensemble)
'I'm a bad, bad man' (Frank and girls)
'Doin' what comes natur'lly' (Annie, Kids and Wilson)
'The girl that I marry' (Frank)
'You can't get a man with a gun' (Annie)
'There's no business like show business' (Charlie, Buffalo Bill, Frank and Annie)
'They say it's wonderful' (Frank and Annie)
'Moonshine lullaby' (Annie and porters)
'My defences are down' (Frank and chorus)
'I'm an Indian, too' (Annie)

Act 2   'I got lost in his arms' (Annie and ensemble)
'Who do you love, I hope?' (Tommy and Winnie)
'I got the sun in the morning' (Annie and ensemble)
'Anything you can do, I can do better' (Annie and Frank)

Anything Goes, *a musical comedy in two acts. Music and lyrics by Cole Porter, book by Guy Bolton and P. G. Wodehouse, revised by Howard Lindsay and Russel Crouse. First produced: New York, 1934; London, 1935. Set in New York, on a transatlantic liner, and in England in contemporary period.* (Performing rights: Samuel French Ltd.)

Reno Lagrange, on board a liner taking her to England to

perform in nightclubs, encounters her New York boy friend, Billy Croker. He had come to see her off, but found that another passenger is his former fiancée, Hope Harcourt, who is heading for England and marriage with Sir Evelyn Oakleigh. Billy impulsively decided to stay on board, and has been able to do so without being branded a stowaway through a chance meeting with a little clergyman, Dr Moon, who is in reality a gangster, 'Public Enemy No. 13', quitting the States in disguise. His confederate, 'Public Enemy No. 1', Snake-Eyes Johnson, having failed to turn up, he has given the man's ticket and passport to Billy. Billy is able to enjoy the voyage alternating between his two girl friends, and goes untroubled by Moon's arrest and detention.

When they reach England, Hope travels to her fiancé's home heavy-hearted, for neither she nor he wishes the marriage, which has been arranged so that her family's money will save a business concern with which both sides are associated. But it turns out that there is no financial crisis after all, thus Hope is free to return to the willing Billy and Sir Evelyn to pursue his speedily conceived interest in Reno; while even 'Dr Moon' is told that the police do not want him after all.

PRINCIPAL NUMBERS

Act 1   'I get a kick out of you' (Reno)
        'All through the night' (Hope and Billy)
        'You're the top' (Billy and Reno)
        'Anything goes' (Reno)
Act 2   'Blow, Gabriel, blow' (Reno and chorus)
        'Be like a bluebird' (Dr Moon)
        'The gypsy in me' (Hope)

The Arcadians, *a fantastic musical play in three acts. Music by Lionel Monckton and Howard Talbot, book by Mark Ambient, Alexander M. Thompson and Robert Courtneidge, lyrics by Arthur Wimperis. First produced: London, 1909. Set in Arcady and England in contemporary period.* (Performing rights: Samuel French Ltd.)

The inhabitants of Arcady, to whom time and care are unknown, receive an unexpected visitor, James Smith, of London, who falls unharmed from an aeroplane. He quickly becomes popular with the Arcadians, but introduces them to such non-Arcadian elements as lying and jealousy. He is accordingly purified in the Well of Truth, renamed Simplicitas, and sent with two girls, Sombra and Chrysea, to persuade the heathen English to mend their ways.

They find themselves at Askwood racecourse where the Corinthian Stakes are about to be run. A young owner, Jack Meadows, has put all his money on his own horse, The Deuce, which is to be ridden by his doleful jockey, Peter Doody. Jack's Irish sweetheart, Eileen Cavanagh, is the niece of James Smith's wife, who is there in charge of the catering, but Simplicitas passes unrecognized. When Doody is injured by his mettlesome mount, Simplicitas takes his place and, thanks to Sombra's ability to speak to animals and thus instruct The Deuce what to do, wins the race handsomely.

Simplicitas opens a restaurant in London and is soon doing a roaring trade. Little progress is being made in the mission of conversion, however, and romantic complications are setting in, due to Eileen's suspicions that Jack Meadows is becoming attached to Sombra. It is Sombra who heals the breach by lecturing them on the evils of jealousy. Unfortunately for Simplicitas's Arcadian pretensions, Mrs Smith, who has become very attracted to him, suddenly detects that his voice is much like her own Jim's, and that if only he had the whiskers her Jim had had when she last saw him he might be the same person. Simplicitas denies ever having had whiskers, and this outright lie immediately disqualifies him as an Arcadian. He is restored to his wife, and Sombra and Chrysea return to their own, better, land.

PRINCIPAL NUMBERS

Act 1 'Arcadians are we' (Chorus)
      'The pipes of Pan' (Sombra)
Act 2 'The girl with a brogue' (Eileen)
      'This is really altogether too provoking' (Chorus)
      'Far away in Arcady' (Sombra)
      'You're taking such good care of me' (Eileen and Jack)
      'The horses are out' (Chorus)
Act 3 'When first I came to London Town' (Chrysea)
      'I've gotter motto, always merry and bright' (Doody)
      'When I wander in my garden' (Eileen and chorus)

The Belle of New York, *a musical comedy in two acts. Music by Gustav Kerker, book and lyrics by Hugh Morton, rewritten in 1927 by Ernest Hendrie and in 1957 by Bernard Dunn and Emile Littler. First produced: New York, 1897; London, 1898. Set in New York in contemporary period.* (Performing rights: Samuel French Ltd.)

Harry Bronson, aged twenty-one and about to be married to the 'Queen of Comic Opera', Cora Angelique, during the convenient absence of his moralizing father, is enjoying a final stag party. It does not remain 'stag' for long, however, for there arrives an old flame of Harry's, Kissy Fitzgarter, with a low comedian, Kenneth Mugg. Then a little Parisienne named Fifi springs out of the giant wedding cake, and Harry falls for her at once.

A less welcome arrival, just as the wedding itself is about to begin, is Harry's father, Ichabod Bronson, at the head of his uniformed Anti-Cigarette Brigade. Later a well-mannered lunatic, Karl, brandishes a knife with which he intends to kill Mr Bronson. He is restrained, and finally blows himself up. Bronson carries out his threat to disown his son. He decides to devote his millions instead to helping Violet Gray, an old friend's daughter, who is a staunch Salvation Army worker.

Though pursued by Fifi, Harry falls truly in love with Violet, who is not unaware of her own charms. Concluding that doing good goes all the better for looking chic, she places herself at the head of a new organization, the Ornamental Purity Brigade. Harry does not mind her having his father's money, but she thinks it unfair to him and tries to shock Bronson Snr by pretending to be a 'saucy' girl named Bonnebouche. Bronson is actually delighted with her, and gladly allows her to marry his son. The discarded Cora marries the comedian Mugg, Bronson Snr helps himself to Pansy, a soubrette, and the only one left uncoupled is Fifi. (In a later version Fifi is offered the post of Ichabod's 'secretary' – with prospects of a happy future.)

PRINCIPAL NUMBERS

Act 1   'When a man is twenty-one' (Chorus)
'When I was born the stars stood still' (Cora and chorus)
'Teach me how to kiss' (Fifi)
'The Anti-Cigarette Society' (Bronson Snr)
'*La belle Parisienne*' (Fifi and bridesmaids)
'They all follow me' (Violet)
'She is the Belle of New York' (Blinky Bill)
Act 2   'When we are married' (Fifi and Harry)
'The Purity Brigade' (Violet and chorus)
'On the beach at Narragansett' (Bronson Snr)
'At the naughty Folies Bergère' (Violet)

Bitter Sweet, *an operetta in three acts. Music, book and lyrics by Noël Coward. First produced: London, 1929. Set in London in 1929, with 'flashbacks' to London in 1875 and 1895, and Vienna in 1880.* (Performing rights: Samuel French Ltd.)

The guests at a dance in a fashionable London house in 1929 have departed to supper, leaving the band-leader, Vincent Howard, musing at the piano. His thoughts are interrupted by the arrival of an engaged couple, Henry

Jekyll and Dolly Chamberlain, who are bickering. When Henry leaves crossly, Vincent, who has been having an affaire with Dolly, takes the opportunity to kiss her a passionate farewell. This is witnessed by the hostess, Lady Shayne, to whom it recalls her own past, which is seen in flashback.

In 1875, Lady Shayne, then Sarah Millick, had fallen in love with her Austrian singing teacher, Carl Linden. Despite her engagement to another man, she had eloped with Carl to Vienna, where they had married and found work in a café: Carl leads the band and Sarah acts as a dance hostess, encouraging the male customers to spend their money. Although she is happy with Carl, Sarah's job is anathema to her. An Austrian officer, Captain Lutte, who has been unable to progress with her as far as he wishes, complains to the proprietor, Herr Schlick. Schlick tries to force Sarah to entertain Lutte in a private room. She refuses and Carl agrees to take her away to Budapest, where they will start a little café of their own. Lutte insults Sarah. Carl attacks him and they fight with swords, with the result that the unskilled Carl is killed.

Fifteen years later, Sarah, now a famous singer, is introduced to guests at the London house of the Marquess of Shayne, who has fallen in love with her. The guests prove to be her ex-fiancé and all the others who had been present at her parents' house on the night she had eloped with Carl. Although she can never love anyone after Carl, she agrees to do her best to make Lord Shayne happy, and the scene moves forward finally to 1929, with Vincent Howard playing one of Lady's Shayne's most famous songs in modern tempo, while Dolly Chamberlain stands thoughtfully at his side.

Act 1 'The call of life' (Lady Shayne)
'If you could only come with me' (Carl)
'I'll see you again' (Carl and Sarah)
Polka
'What is love?' (Sarah and chorus)
'The last dance' (Ensemble)
Act 2 'Ladies of the town' (Lotte, Freda, Hansi and Gussi)
'If love were all' (Manon)
'Dear little café' (Sarah, Carl and chorus)
'Tokay' (Capt Schensi and chorus)
'Kiss me' (Manon)
Act 3 'Ta-ra-ra-bom-' (Chorus)
'Alas the time is past' (Victoria, Harriet, Effie, Gloria, June and Honor)
'Green carnations' (Vincent, Cedric, Bertram and Lord Henry)
'Zigeuner' (Sarah)

Bless the Bride, *a musical play in two acts. Music by Vivian Ellis, book and lyrics by A. P. Herbert. First produced: London, 1947. Set in England and France in 1870.* (Performing rights: Emile Littler Musical Plays.)

At the home of the Willow family at Mayfield, Sussex, preparations for the marriage next day of one of the six daughters, Lucy, to the Hon. Thomas Trout have given way temporarily to a game of croquet. Thomas is bored and fetches from the local inn two French friends of his, Pierre Fontaine and Suzanne Valois, an actor and actress, whom he introduces as Monsieur and Madame Fontaine of the French Embassy. Lucy's father invites them to attend his and his wife's golden wedding party that evening. They accept readily, Pierre especially, for he has already fallen head over heels in love with Lucy, whom he overwhelms with the way he kisses, and informs that he is not married to Suzanne at all. At the party he begs Lucy to elope with him, but although she does not wish to marry Thomas she dare not defy her parents. Suzanne, who is jealous of Pierre's attention to Lucy, overhears their conversation.

On her wedding morning Lucy becomes increasingly upset at the prospect. She is rescued by Pierre, disguised as a doctor, who carries her off, sending a message to the church that she has been taken ill, and leaving her pageboy, disguised in her wedding dress and veil, for her outraged family to find.

Pierre and Lucy make their way to Eauville-sur-mer in France, closely followed by Suzanne, who will not leave them alone. Lucy's mother and father (Mary and Augustus) arrive in search of them, with Thomas Trout and Lucy's cousin George, the men not very well disguised as Frenchmen. The Franco-Prussian War is imminent, so these eccentric foreigners are quickly suspected of being German spies and have to be rescued from the attentions of the police in a restaurant by Lucy. They order her to return home with them. Pierre, a reservist officer, has to leave to join his regiment, and Lucy sadly accompanies her parents back to Sussex.

There they learn through Suzanne that Pierre has been killed. Lucy falls into a state of brooding over her lost love, and gently tells the persistent Thomas Trout that she can never love him nor anyone else. It is Lucy's twenty-first birthday, and one of the visitors arriving with a present is Suzanne. The gift is Pierre, about whose death in action Suzanne had lied out of jealousy. Thomas gracefully surrenders Lucy to the only man she could ever love.

PRINCIPAL NUMBERS

Act 1   'Too good to be true' (Thomas and Lucy)
        'Any man but Thomas Trout' (Lucy)
        '*En Angleterre, les demoiselles*' (Suzanne, Pierre and Thomas)
        'I was never kissed before' (Lucy, Pierre and Suzanne)
        'The silent heart' (Lucy)
        '*Ma belle Marguerite*' (Pierre and chorus)
        'God bless the family' (Augustus, Mary, Nanny, Lucy and chorus)
Act 2 '*Mon pauvre petit Pierre*' (Suzanne, Lucy and Pierre)
        'The Englishman' (Mary, Augustus, Thomas and George)
        'A table for two' (Pierre)
        'This is my lovely day' (Lucy and Pierre)
        'My big moment' (Thomas)

Brigadoon, *a musical play in two acts. Music by Frederick Loewe, book and lyrics by Alan Jay Lerner. First produced: New York, 1947; London, 1949. Set in the Scottish Highlands and New York in 1935.* (Performing rights: Sam Fox Publishing Company.)

Brigadoon is the name of a Scottish Highland village which unaccountably appears for only one day each hundred years. Its 20th-century manifestation happens to be witnessed by two American tourists, Tommy Albright and Jeff Douglas, who are wandering about lost at the time. Unaware that there is anything strange about the village, they find themselves in its main square, populated by a throng who appear all too normal in their traits of character and passion. The presence of strangers interrupts their proceedings briefly, but it is not long before Tommy Albright, who has taken an immediate fancy to one of the girls, Fiona MacLaren, is going off hand-in-hand with her to pick heather for her sister Jean's imminent wedding to Charlie Dalrymple.

The Americans still do not know that there is anything supernatural about Brigadoon and its folk, but they are aware that there is something unusual about the place. Fiona will not say what it is, so they question an aged inhabitant and learn the strange story. They stay to see the wedding. It is as well for the bride and groom that they do, for when a jealous rival of Charlie Dalrymple, Harry Beaton, tries to stab Charlie it is Jeff Douglas who trips him up, causing him to fall fatally.

Tommy speaks of his determination to stay in Brigadoon for ever and marry Fiona, but Jeff convinces him that he must face up to real life and return to his fiancée, Jane Ashton, in New York. Tommy and Fiona part sadly and Brigadoon returns to oblivion for another century. Back in New York, however, an expression Jane Ashton uses conjures up for Tommy a vision of Fiona. He cannot wait to return to Scotland to find out, once and for all, whether Brigadoon is fact or fantasy. Jeff goes with him. Sure enough, there is no Brigadoon to be found, but before Tommy can turn unhappily away they hear a voice hailing them. It is the old inhabitant, come to assure them that love is potent enough to work miracles, and to lead Tommy by the hand to his own love, Fiona.

PRINCIPAL NUMBERS

Prologue   'Once in the Highlands' (Chorus)
          'Brigadoon' (Chorus)
Act 1   'Waitin' for my dearie' (Fiona and girls)
          'I'll go home with bonnie Jean' (Charlie and chorus)
          'The heather on the hill' (Fiona and Tommy)
          'The love of my life' (Meg)
          'Jeannie's packin' up' (Chorus)
          'Come to me, bend to me' (Charlie)
          'Almost like being in love' (Fiona and Tommy)
          'Entrance of the Clans'
          Sword Dance and Reel
Act 2   'Run an' get 'im!' (Chorus)
          'There but for you go I' (Tommy)
          'My mother's weddin' day' (Meg)
          Funeral: traditional Piobrachead
          'From this day on' (Fiona and Tommy)

Call Me Madam, *a musical in two acts. Music and lyrics by Irving Berlin, book by Howard Lindsay and Russel Crouse. First produced: New York, 1950; London, 1952. Set in Washington and the Grand Duchy of Lichtenburg in contemporary period.* (Performing rights: Irving Berlin Ltd.)

The American Ambassador to Lichtenburg – a woman – is being sworn in. She is Mrs Sally Adams, a brash, handsome

27

widow who attributes her appointment to having been 'the hostess with the mostes' on the ball'. She appoints a young official, Kenneth Gibson, her private secretary and carries him off to Lichtenburg, where she proceeds to flaunt her authority by instructing the *Chargé d'Affaires* at the Embassy to call her Madam, and refusing the Foreign Secretary an American Government loan.

Her tactics are soon changed when a new Foreign Secretary, Cosmo Constantine, proves so attractive that she immediately falls in love with him and presses him to accept a huge sum of dollars for his country. To her chagrin he refuses, declaring that Lichtenburg must work out its destiny unaided. When she arranges the loan over his head he resigns, bringing about the first general election for twenty years, one beneficial result of which is that the heir to the throne, Princess Maria, who has fallen in love with Kenneth Gibson, finds herself free at last from her duty and can propose to him: he accepts.

A party of Congressmen, sent to investigate Sally's doings, reports adversely and she is recalled to the United States, Kenneth remaining in Lichtenburg to marry Maria and devote himself to building a hydro-electric plant which his father has financed. Back in Washington, Sally tries to save face by reassuming command of society life. She seems likely to fail, but is saved by the arrival of Cosmo Constantine, now Prime Minister, who has been sent by the Grand Duke to invest Sally with a decoration for her services to his country. Their reunion is obviously going to be a permanent one.

Can-Can, *a musical play in two acts. Music and lyrics by Cole Porter, from the book by Abe Burrows. First produced: New York, 1953; London, 1954. Set in Paris in 1893.* (Performing rights: Evans Plays.)

The plot of the play is subsidiary to the songs and dances. The principal setting is a café in the Montmartre district, owned by a ravishingly commanding creature, Pistache. Her trade depends largely on that most uninhibited of dances, the Can-Can, which is the surreptitious rage of Paris, having been banned by the authorities. A new young judge, Aristide Forestier, is sent to the café to investigate rumours that the prohibited dance is still flourishing. Pistache knows why he has come and proceeds to beguile him, with such success that he is soon madly in love with her and only too willing to find ways to save her from judicial wrath and enable her café to continue its joy-giving

29

entertainment. He succeeds and gains Pistache for his reward.

An interwoven story concerns some of the artistic denizens of Montmartre, including Boris, Hercule, Hilaire, Étienne, Théophile and others.

PRINCIPAL NUMBERS

Act 1   'Maidens typical of France' (Chorus)
'Never give anything away' (Pistache and girls)
'C'est magnifique' (Pistache and Aristide)
'Come along with me' (Hilaire)
'Live and let live' (Pistache)
'I'm in love' (Aristide)
'If you loved me truly' (Claudine, Boris, Théophile, Hercule, Étienne, Gabrielle, Celestine, Marie and model)
'Montmartre' (Chorus)
Garden of Eden Ballet and Eve's Dance
'Allez-vous-en' (Pistache)

Act 2   'Never, never be an artist' (Boris, Hercule, Étienne, Théophile and model)
'It's all right with me' (Aristide)
'Every man is a stupid man' (Pistache)
'I love Paris' (Pistache and chorus)
'Can-Can' (Pistache and chorus)

A Chinese Honeymoon, *a musical comedy in two acts. Music by Howard Talbot, book and lyrics by George Dance. First produced: London, 1901. Set in China in contemporary period.* (Performing rights: Chappell & Co. Ltd.)

The Emperor of China, Ylang Ylang, wishes to find an

Empress who can combine suitably imperial qualities with an undivided love for him as a man. To this end he sends his Lord High Admiral, Hi Lung, on an extensive search, promising him his niece Soo-Soo if he succeeds. This prospect appeals to Hi Lung – who, it happens, is English – and he pursues his quest vigorously, for he knows that the Lord Chancellor, too, has his eye on Soo-Soo. But all Hi Lung's efforts are in vain, and he returns from visiting ninety-seven ports with his mission unaccomplished.

Another man in love with Soo-Soo is Tom Hatherton, an English gentleman of leisure. Soo-Soo has been absenting herself from the palace, posing as a singer, in order to meet him. Complications are caused by the arrival of the Pineapple family: Mr Pineapple is curious to find out why Tom is no longer in the army. A friendly waitress disguises Tom as a doctor, who promptly 'examines' Soo-Soo and orders a long voyage for the good of her health, intending to join her on it. Various side plots tangle things further, but, of course, everyone pairs off happily by the end.

PRINCIPAL NUMBERS

Act 1   'A paper fan' (Soo-Soo)
          'A Chinese honeymoon' (Marie, Pineapple, Flo, Violet, Millie and Gerti)
          'The à la girl' (Mrs Pineapple)
          'The twiddly bits' (Fi-Fi)
Act 2   'I want to be a lidy' (Fi-Fi)
          'Daisy with the dimple' (Soo-Soo)
          'That happy land' (Pineapple)
          'Roses red and white' (Soo-Soo and Tom)
          'Martha spanks the grand pianner' (Fi-Fi)

Chu Chin Chow, *a musical tale of the East in two acts,* *'told' by Oscar Asche with music by Frederic Norton. First* *produced: London, 1916. Set in Persia in about the 9th* *century, the time of the* Arabian Nights *story 'Ali Baba* *and the Forty Thieves', on which it is partly based.* (Performing rights: Samuel French Ltd.)

The wealthy merchant Kasim Baba has not been lucky in his guests. Four times, after visitors have left, his palace has been robbed; but he has plenty of resources left and, undeterred, awaits a further guest, a Shanghai merchant named Chu Chin Chow. Little does Kasim Baba know that this is the same man who has visited him four times before, in different guises, and that he is really Abu Hasan, the notorious leader of a band of forty villains.

The one person in Kasim Baba's palace who does know the secret is a female slave, Zahrat Al-Kulub. She is Abu Hasan's spy, but is only awaiting her chance to break free from his dominance. Two other women seeking freedom – in their case from Kasim Baba – are Alcolom, his wife, and Marjanah, another of his slaves. Zahrat Al-Kulub tells them the secret of Abu Hasan, alias Chu Chin Chow, and suggests that Marjanah should approach him and threaten to reveal his identity unless he will buy her and set her free and also murder Kasim Baba, thus providing Alcolom with the freedom of widowhood.

Abu Hasan arrives with his followers and Marjanah loses no time in putting her proposition to him. He has to agree to it, but realizes that Zahrat Al-Kulub must have betrayed him, and vows to 'reward' her. Abu Hasan's attempt to purchase Marjanah is thwarted by Ali Baba, Kasim's brother, who drunkenly insists on outbidding the visitor for her, so Marjanah and her lover, Nur Al-Huda, decide to escape. Together with Ali Baba they keep a rendezvous next morning in a rocky place outside the city, where they are astonished to hear a subterranean cry of 'Open, Sesame!', and to see Abu Hasan and his men emerge from the ground singing, causing the rocky door to close behind them by ordering it to 'Shut, Sesame!' When the robbers have gone the eavesdroppers use the same formula to enter the cave, in which they find a vast hoard of money and treasure. They take enough to re-compense Ali Baba for his reckless purchase of Marjanah, and leave.

At the palace Abu Hasan buys all the slaves, including Zahrat Al-Kulub, whom he immediately orders to be kept chained for ever in his cave. She retaliates by dis-closing his identity to everyone, but he merely calls in his forty thieves and forces the other merchants to hand over all their gold.

Ali Baba tells his brother Kasim Baba the secret of the cave. Kasim hastens there, is surprised by Abu Hasan, and hacked into pieces. But later Abu Hasan finds the remains missing, and Zahrat Al-Kulub, who had been chained to a stake in the cave, vanishes. (He is not to know that Marjanah and Nur Al-Huda were responsible for this.) In Baghdad he meets Zahrat Al-Kulub, who checks his fury by proposing a plan which delights him with its possibilities for mayhem at the wedding of Nur Al-Huda and Marjanah next evening. He is to attend as an oil merchant, bringing with him forty large jars, in each of which one of his followers will be hidden. When he sings a song, 'The Scimitar', the men will leap out with their swords and cut everyone down.

The preparations are duly made, but while Abu Hasan

is absent Zahrat Al-Kulub's henchman, Abdullah, who had been Kasim Baba's major-domo, carries out her orders to have boiling oil poured into each jar, while a gay song drowns the screams of the dying thieves. When Abu Hasan sings his song there are no followers left to respond. Instead, he is stabbed to death by Zahrat Al-Kulub, and the wedding party is resumed with increased rejoicing.

PRINCIPAL NUMBERS

Act 1 'Here be oysters' (Abdullah and chorus)
'I am Chu Chin Chow'
'Cleopatra's Nile' (Marjanah and chorus)
'I'll sing and dance' (Ali Baba)
Serenade: 'Corraline' (Nur Al-Huda and Marjanah)
'When a pullet is plump' (Ali Baba)
'We are the robbers of the woods' (Robber band)
'I love thee so' (Marjanah)
'All my days till the end of my life' (Marjanah and Ali Baba)

Act 2 'I long for the sun' (Alcolom)
'Mahbubah' (Marjanah, Nur Al-Huda, Alcolom)
'I built a fairy palace in the sky' (Marjanah)
'The Scimitar' (Abu Hasan)
'Any time's kissing time' (Alcolom)
'The cobbler's song' (Baba Mustapha)
'How dear is our day' (Alcolom and Ali Baba)
'Olive oil' (Abdullah and chorus)

34

The Cingalee, *a musical play in two acts. Music by Lionel Monckton, with additional numbers by Paul A. Rubens, book by James T. Tanner, lyrics by Adrian Ross and Percy Greenbank. First produced: London, 1904. Set in Ceylon in contemporary period.* (Performing rights: Emile Littler Musical Plays.)

The Hon. Harry Vereker, an English tea-planter in Ceylon, has rented a plantation from a lawyer, Chambhuddy Ram. The transaction is a fraudulent one, for the plantation belongs to a Cingalese girl, Nanoya, who is working on it as an ordinary labourer in order to escape the consequences of her betrothal in infancy to an overbearing nobleman, Boobhamba Chettur Bhoy.

By the time Boobhamba has tracked her down, Nanoya has fallen in love with Harry. Sir Peter Loftus, who combines the functions of British High Commissioner and Judge, is appealed to by Boobhamba and decrees that Nanoya must marry him.

From Peggy Sabine, a teacher of calisthenics, Harry comes into possession of a black pearl of great value, which he presents to Nanoya, not knowing that it had been stolen in the first place by the rascally Chambhuddy Ram. When Sir Peter, who has been tracking down Chambhuddy, accuses him of the theft, the lawyer is able to deny that the pearl is in his possession, and to point to Nanoya as the thief. Her only means of saving herself is to go through with her marriage to Boobhamba, a fate from which she is saved at the eleventh hour by Harry, disguised as a rickshaw-boy and aided and abetted by Peggy Sabine and Lady Patricia.

Act 1   'Pearl of sweet Ceylon' (Harry)
'Tea, tea, tea' (Naitoomba and Tea Girls)
'Hail the noble' (Boobhamba)
'My heart's at your feet' (Lady Patricia)
'Four little girls of Ceylon' (Warren and Tea Girls)
'In the island of gay Ceylon' (Patricia, Peggy, Angy, Boobhamba, Sir Peter and Warren)
'Cinnamon tree' (Nanoya and chorus)

Act 2   'The dance I'll lead him' (Nanoya and Tea Girls)
'The wonderful English pot' (Chambhuddy)
'My dear little Cingalee' (Harry)
'You and I and I and you' (Lady Patricia and Warren)
'Gollywogs' (Peggy and Chambhuddy)
'Sloe eyes' (Nanoya)

A Country Girl, *a musical play in two acts. Music by Lionel Monckton, with additional numbers by Paul A. Rubens, book by James T. Tanner, lyrics by Adrian Ross and Percy Greenbank. First produced: London, 1894. Set in Devonshire and London in contemporary period.* (Performing rights: Emile Littler Musical Plays.)

At the height of Parliamentary election fever in this rose-entwined Devonshire village there comes the additional excitement of the return of the popular young squire, Commander Geoffrey Challoner, R.N., from service abroad. His resourceful manservant, Barry, immediately presses his master to stand as candidate. Although Geoffrey

36

has no money and many misgivings, he yields, as always, to Barry, who assures him he will organize everything.

The village is filling rapidly; another arrival is Marjorie Joy, whom Geoffrey has loved since childhood, returning from London as a successful singer; and there follow the elderly White Rajah of Bhong and his fiancée, the attractive Princess Mehelaneh. This gives rise to some complications, for the Rajah is actually Quentin Raikes, who had vanished in the Himalayas some years before and whose wife is the most prominent lady in this very village; and Princess Meheleneh, far from loving the Rajah, is only interested in Geoffrey Challoner, whom she had met on board ship.

Geoffrey tells Nan, a village girl, that he loves Marjorie, but he rounds off the assurance with a friendly kiss, which Marjorie sees and misinterprets. He manages to explain things to her, only to be seen in due course kissing the Princess. Marjorie is not to know that he had just declined the Princess's invitation to marry her and take up a lotus-eating life in Bhong. He has kissed one person too many, and Marjorie sadly leaves the village. The Princess seizes the opportunity to repeat her offer, only to be rejected again.

At a period-dress ball in London, Geoffrey, now a Member of Parliament, is introduced to Marjorie under her professional name, Miss Montague. Although he does not recognize her in her costume, her resemblance to his lost sweetheart causes him to pour out confidences about his true love. Reassured at last, Marjorie, when invited to sing, chooses a song they had shared in childhood, and they are soon in one another's arms.

Act 1 'Try again, Johnnie' (Nan and chorus)
      'Coo' (Marjorie)
      'Yo ho! Little girls, yo ho!' (Barry and chorus)
      'Boy and girl' (Marjorie and Geoffrey)
      'The Rajah of Bhong' (Rajah and Princess)
      'Molly the Marchioness' (Nan)
      'Two little chicks' (Sophie and Barry)
      'Under the Deodar' (Princess)
Act 2 'The sailor man' (Geoffrey and chorus)
      'Me and Mrs Brown' (Barry and girls)
      'My own little girl' (Geoffrey)
      'Quarrelling' (Sophie and Barry)
      'Take your pretty partner' (Nan, Marjorie, Sophie,
         Rajah, Douglas and Lord Grassmere)

The Dancing Mistress, *a musical play in three acts. Music by Lionel Monckton, book by James T. Tanner, lyrics by Adrian Ross and Percy Greenbank. First produced: London, 1912. Set in England and Switzerland in contemporary period.* (Performing rights: Emile Littler Musical Plays.)

Another of those shows whose story-line can convey nothing of their overall charm, *The Dancing Mistress* is about Nancy Joyce, a winning girl just about to leave finishing school, whose headmistress invites her to stay on and teach dancing. She accepts. Her best friend there, Bella Peach, has a cousin, Teddy Cavanagh, whose arrival quickly makes Nancy glad she has stayed. Bella, for her part, is enjoying herself increasingly with the riding master.

A Baron Montalba sponsors Teddy on an aeroplane flight across the Alps. The attempt fails, and Teddy meets up with an old flame in Switzerland, causing some complications with Nancy. But these are happily sorted out back in England, and Teddy and Nancy are brought back to each other.

PRINCIPAL NUMBERS

Act 1	'Tom, Dick and Harry' (Bella and chorus)
	'Cantering' (Bella, Jeannie, Lyndale and Widdicombe)
	'The dancing mistress' (Nancy)
	'Fly-away-Jack' (Nancy and Teddy)
Act 2	'I'm having a richt guid time' (Jeannie)
	'When you're in love' (Baron)
	'If I were to dance like you' (Nancy and Teddy)
	'Dance, little snowflake' (Nancy)
Act 3	'Ev'ry woman' (Nancy)
	'Ninette' (Bella)
	'Not at present' (Jeannie and Widdicombe)

The Dancing Years, *a musical play in three acts. Music by Ivor Novello, lyrics by Christopher Hassall. First produced: London, 1939. Set in Austria from 1911–38.* (Performing rights: Samuel French Ltd.)

In 1911, Rudi Kleber, a composer of operettas, is having a playful romance with his landlady's niece, fifteen-year-old Grete Schöne, when he meets the famous singer Maria Zeigler, who at once falls for him. She carries him off to compose for her and live in the palace of her admirer,

Prince Charles Metterling; but before he leaves, Rudi promises Grete that he will give her the chance to accept or refuse him before he commits himself to marry anyone else.

Rudi's new work, *Lorelei*, is produced some months later, with Maria and her singing teacher, Cäcilie Kurt, making a big success in it. Afterwards, Maria refuses to receive Prince Charles, entertaining Rudi privately instead. Charles intrudes and insults Rudi, but fails to dampen his growing ardour for Maria. In fact, three years later Maria and Rudi are found living together happily, though unmarried, in the Tyrol.

Grete, who has meanwhile made her name as a dancer in England, arrives back in Austria a sophisticated young woman. Maria is at once jealous of Rudi's affectionate greeting for her, not knowing that Grete has acquired an earnest admirer of her own, a young officer named Franzl. Maria summons Prince Charles, who lives nearby, and confides in him that she is going to have Rudi's child. Charles reaffirms his offer to marry her. Maria is touched, but still feels more strongly for Rudi, until she hears him make a mock proposal to Grete (which she rejects) to honour his old promise.

Maria marries Prince Charles, leaving Rudi desolate. He does not meet her again until twelve years later, in a Vienna restaurant. They know their love is as strong as ever, and Maria is not happy with Charles. However, when Rudi urges her to run away with him she introduces their son, who has grown up believing the Prince to be his father, pointing out that a disruption now could wreck the boy's life. Rudi sadly agrees, and they part for ever.

Act 1   'Waltz of my heart' (Officers and girls)
        A Masque of Venice (Part I)
        'The wings of sleep' (Maria and Cäcilie Kurt)
        'My life belongs to you' (Ceruti)
        'I can give you the starlight' (Maria)
Act 2   'My dearest dear' (Maria)
        Chorale and Tyrolese Dance
        'Primrose' (Grete)
        A Masque of Venice (Part II)
        'In praise of love' (Pelotti, Sadun, Cäcilie, Ceruti
          and Valdo)
        The Leap Year Waltz
        A Masque of Venice (Part III)

Derby Day, *a comic opera in three acts. Music by Alfred Reynolds, book and lyrics by A. P. Herbert. First produced: London, 1932. Set in the Epsom vicinity in contemporary period.* (Performing rights: Elkin & Company Limited.)

It is the eve of the Derby. Bert Bones, a Cockney tipster, loves Rose, barmaid of the Old Black Horse, but cannot declare himself eloquently enough. One who can, and does, is Eddy Waters, the son of the local bigwig, Sir Horace Waters. Not realizing that he is merely amusing himself with her, Rose broaches the matter of marriage. Eddy pleads the poverty of a young man still at university, so she decides to raise money for them by putting £100, borrowed from her employer's safe, on to Sir Horace's horse, Pericles, who is favourite for the great race.

When Sir Horace informs John Bitter, the landlord, that

the local Justices have decided not to renew his licence, Bert Bones suggests to Bitter that they 'nobble' Pericles in revenge. Their method of doing this is to hiss insults at the animal, who is intelligent enough to be upset by them. Rose also visits the horse, to plead charmingly with it to win, and Sir Horace comes on the same mission. All this confuses Pericles, who faints away. The Derby is run and won by the new favourite, losing Rose her misappropriated £100 but making Bert a small fortune.

John Bitter proposes marriage to Mrs Bones, Bert's mother, who accepts him. Sir Horace and his brother Justices pay a surprise visit to the Old Black Horse, during which Rose's theft is discovered. Bert tries to take the blame, but she insists on telling the truth, which causes everyone to round on Sir Horace and accuse him of corrupting an innocent girl by owning racehorses for her to bet upon. The aged Justices call for beer and proceed to make merry, Sir Horace restores the pub's licence, and Rose helps Bert to make her his proposal of marriage at last.

PRINCIPAL NUMBERS

Act 1   'Nothing's been the same' (Mrs Bones)
        'Who wants a winner?' (Bert and chorus)
        'Somethin' for nothin'' (John Bitter and chorus)
        'I want to be a lady' (Rose)
        'Angels were busy' (Eddy)
        'Take me away' (Rose, Eddy and Bert)
        'The radish and the swede' (Lady and Sir Horace Waters)

The Desert Song, *a musical play in two acts. Music by Sigmund Romberg, book and lyrics by Otto Harbach, Oscar Hammerstein II and Frank Mandel. First produced: New York, 1926; London, 1927. Set in French Morocco in contemporary period.* (Performing rights: Samuel French Ltd.)

The French in Morocco are having trouble with bandits, the Riffs. Even so, a young lieutenant, Pierre Birabeau, the General's son, can feel some pity for them, having witnessed his colonel's cruelty towards them. Although he is a mild young man he remonstrates with his superior, who forgets himself and strikes Pierre. From this moment Pierre proceeds to live a double life, as French officer and as Red Shadow, the Riffs' leader.

As Pierre he is known to be in love with Margot Bonvalet, the daughter of the provincial Governor, who is the fiancée of Captain Paul Fontaine. Margot is fond of Pierre, but longs for real romance. One day the Red Shadow raids the Governor's house and carries Margot off to a desert palace and makes passionate love to her. He tries to persuade her to live the desert life with him, but she insists that Pierre is the man she loves. Chivalrously, Red Shadow offers to bring Pierre to her, and, indeed, he shortly enters; but after the ardour of the bandit, Margot is

43

disappointed to find Pierre uninspiring. He goes and Red Shadow returns, to resume the love-making to which she now responds eagerly.

General Birabeau has been leading a force in search of Margot. When they swarm into the palace and the General advances towards Red Shadow with drawn sword the bandit leader refuses to defend himself. He is declared a common outlaw and his tribe cast him out into the desert, with a minimum of food, to be hunted to death by French Légionnaires on the unwitting orders of his own father. It is only when a dancing girl, Azuri, discloses the secret she has learned – that Red Shadow is Pierre Birabeau, and that he had not defended himself because he could not fight his own father – that the General realizes what he has done. Pierre returns, claiming to have 'finished' the Red Shadow himself, and is welcomed by all; not least Margot, overjoyed to find that Pierre and her tempestuous desert lover are one and the same.

Light relief is provided during the piece by Benny, an incompetent newspaper correspondent, and his secretary Susan, who is sick with love but doesn't possess that essential quality known as 'It'.

PRINCIPAL NUMBERS

Act 1 'The Riff Song' (Red Shadow and Riffs)
'Margot' (Paul and soldiers)
French military marching song: 'Oh girls, girls, here are cavaliers' (Margot and girls)
'Romance' (Margot)
'Then you will know' (Margot and Pierre)
'It' (Susan, Benny and girls)
'The Desert Song' ('One alone') (Margot and Red Shadow)

Act 2　'Song of the brass key' (Clementina and girls)
　　　Spanish Dance
　　　'One good boy gone wrong' (Clementina and
　　　　Benny)
　　　'Let love go'
　　　'One flower in your garden' } (Red Shadow and
　　　'One alone'　　　　　　　 　　others)
　　　'The Sabre Song' (Margot and Red Shadow)

Dorothy, *a comedy opera in three acts. Music by Alfred Cellier, book and lyrics by B. C. Stephenson, based on Aphra Behn's play* The City Heiress. *First produced: London, 1886. Set in Kent in 1740.* (Performing rights: Chappell & Co. Ltd.)

Enjoying the 'Harvest Home' celebrations at a Kentish inn in the guise of village girls are Dorothy Bantam and Lydia Hawthorne, daughter and niece of Sir John Bantam, of Chanticleer Hall. Two young gentlemen who have left London to escape their debts are immediately attracted by the girls, and the response is willing. But if the men do not learn the girls' true identity, neither do 'Dorcas' and 'Abigail' discover that one of the newcomers is Sir John's nephew and heir, Geoffrey Wilder, who is on his way to Chanticleer Hall to submit reluctantly to marriage with Dorothy, whom he has never met, in order to get his uncle to pay off his debts; his companion is his friend, Harry Sherwood.

　　Lurcher, a sheriff's officer pursuing them, gets into difficulties with the villagers and is rescued by Geoffrey, in gratitude for which he agrees to help the two men play a trick on Sir John, intended to get him to part with some

45

money without Geoffrey's having to go through with the unwanted marriage. Lurcher arrives at Chanticleer Hall, introducing himself as secretary to the Duke of Berkshire and friend, who are craving a night's hospitality as their carriage has broken down. Sir John welcomes the visitors, who do not recognize Dorothy and Lydia as the village girls. The girls recognize them, however, and are amused to find themselves courted again, this time by different partners.

During the night a robbery is faked, in which the 'Duke of Berkshire' is the only one to have suffered loss – his money. Sir John insists on making it up to his guest. The young men cheerfully leave next morning, in search of their village girls. They receive a challenge to fight a duel with two other young men, who are Dorothy and Lydia dressed up and wishing to test whether the men really mean their avowals of love for 'Dorcas' and 'Abigail'. The test is passed satisfactorily, and Sir John, who has been told the truth by Lurcher, is easily able to insist that Geoffrey marry Dorothy, while Harry marries Lydia for good measure.

PRINCIPAL NUMBERS

Act 1   'Be wise in time, O Phyllis mine' (Dorothy, Lydia and Phyllis)

'We're sorry to delay you' (Dorothy, Lydia, Geoffrey and Harry)

'With such a dainty maid none can compare' (Geoffrey)

'I am the sheriff's faithful man' (Lurcher, Geoffrey and Harry)

'You swear to be good and true' (Dorothy, Lydia, Geoffrey and Harry)

46

Act 2 'Though born a man of high degree' (Geoffrey)
       'Pleasant dreams' (Ensemble)
       'Contentment I give you' (Sir John and chorus)
       'Queen of my heart' (Harry)
       'Are you sure?' (Geoffrey, Harry and Sir John)
Act 3 Ballet
       'The time has come' (Phyllis)

The Earl and the Girl, *a musical comedy in two acts. Music by Ivan Caryll, book by Seymour Hicks, lyrics by Percy Greenbank. First produced: London, 1903. Set in a rural part of England in contemporary period.* (Performing rights: Chappell & Co. Ltd.)

Richard Wargrave, an orphan, has eloped from Paris with Elphin Haye, who possesses a large fortune. He has brought her to England, and they are making for Stole Hall, where her aunt, Miss Virginia Bliss, lives; but at the local inn they are handed a note from that lady warning them that Elphin's uncle and guardian, Bunker Bliss, is furious with them, and urging them to stay away.

While the couple hesitate at the inn they are joined by an old friend of Richard, Crewe Boodle, the American-born heir-apparent to the Earldom of Stole. Crewe is also in trouble, being hounded by a Mrs Shimmering Black, a circus strong-woman, whom he has jilted. Crewe is accompanied by several friends in fancy dress, and all are on their way to a dance at Stole Hall. Richard bribes a comic dog-trainer, Jim Cheese, whom he believes mistakenly to be one of the party, to impersonate him, so that he himself can go to Stole Hall pretending to be Cheese and find out how the land lies.

An American lawyer named Downham is waiting at the Hall for Richard to turn up, having discovered that he, not Crewe Boodle, is the heir. Naturally, he mistakes Jim Cheese for Richard; and at one stage Richard, believed to be Cheese, locks up Bunker Bliss and Mrs Shimmering Black together in a room. The outcome of these and other complications is best summed up as 'all ends happily'.

PRINCIPAL NUMBERS

Act 1 'The sporting girl' (Daisy and chorus)
'Celebrities' (Jim and Liza)
'Shopping' (Daisy and chorus)
'Thou art my rose' (Crewe)
'I haven't a moment to spare' (Downham)
'We were so happy, you and I' (Elphin and Richard)
'When a maiden leaves school' (Elphin and chorus)
'By the shore of the Mediterranean' (Richard and chorus)
For one night only' (Richard, Elphin, Jim and Liza)

Act 2 'The prettiest girl in town' (Daisy)
'Careless Kate' (Elphin)
'I'm a Lord, what ho!' (Jim and chorus)
'My cosy corner girl' (Richard)
'Sammy' (Daisy)
'The Grenadiers' (Crewe and chorus)
'The Queen of June' (Crewe)

The Emerald Isle, *a comic opera in two acts. Music by Arthur Sullivan, completed after his death by Edward German, book and lyrics by Basil Hood. First produced: London, 1901. Set in Ireland in the early 19th century.* (Performing rights: Chappell & Co. Ltd.)

The English Lord Lieutenant of Ireland, the Earl of Newtown, is busily trying to anglicize the Irish; Terence O'Brien, Eton- and Oxford-educated patriot, is working equally hard to resist and reverse the process. The latter engages a Professor Bunn, 'Mesmerist, Ventriloquist, Humorist, Illusionist, Shakespearean Reciter, Character Impersonator and Professor of Elocution', to help him, and orders him to attend the Caves of Carrig-Cleena, the rebels' hideout, for a midnight initiation.

'Blind' Murphy, a fiddler who has never been blind in his life and who is in love with a peasant girl, Molly O'Grady, agrees to play for English soldiers as they march against the rebel headquarters. The news of this impending attack is conveyed to Terence O'Brien by no less than the Lord Lieutenant's daughter, Lady Rosie Pippin, for she and the rebel leader are secretly in love. She believes that Murphy has betrayed the patriots, but Terence inclines to suspect Professor Bunn. The latter proves himself by co-operating in Molly O'Grady's plan to frighten the soldiers away from the caves by making them believe that a fairy lives there who will lure them into becoming her prisoners for life.

The scheme works, but the soldiers remuster and return to the assault. Despite deterrent tactics by Professor Bunn and village girls the rebels are eventually arrested and sentenced to be shot. Terence insists on sharing their fate. Rosie pleads for him, but her father refuses to relent, telling her that the Irishman, in any case, is no suitable match for a girl who has American blood in her veins. Hearing this, Professor Bunn reminds the Lord Lieutenant that America is Ireland's traditional friend, an argument so convincing to the Earl that he cancels the shooting and approves of Terence's and Rosie's union.

PRINCIPAL NUMBERS

Act 1 'Of viceroys we've had' (Murphy and chorus)
'If you wish to appear as an Irish type' (Bunn and chorus)
'On the heights of Glentaun' (Molly, Terence and Murphy)
'Two's company, three's none' (Rosie, Susan, Terence and Bunn)
'At an early stage of life' (Lord Lieutenant, Rosie, Countess and Chaplain)
'When Alfred's friends their king forsook' (Countess)
'Oh setting sun, you bid the world goodbye' (Rosie)
'Now this is the song of the Devonshire men' (Sergeant with chorus)
'Many years ago I strode' (Bunn with chorus)

Act 2 'Bedad, it's for him that will always employ' (Chorus and dance of peasants)
'Oh, have you met a man in debt?' (Terence and chorus)
' 'Twas in Hyde Park' (Rosie and Terence with chorus)
'Oh the age in which we're living' (Bunn)
'Goodbye, my native town' (Murphy)

'I love you! I love you!' (Molly and Murphy)
'There once was a little soldier' (Terence and
chorus)

Florodora, *a musical comedy in two acts. Music by Leslie Stuart, book by Owen Hall, lyrics by E. Boyd-Jones and Paul A. Rubens. First produced: London, 1899. Set in the Philippines and Wales in contemporary period.* (Performing rights: National Operatic and Dramatic Association.)

Florodora is not a girl, but an exotic little island in the Philippines where a celebrated perfume, also named Florodora, is manufactured from a secret recipe. The proprietor of the factory, and thereby 'ruler' of the island, is an American, Cyrus W. Gilfain. He is looking for a chance to marry one of his girl employees, Dolores, for she is the daughter of the deceased owner of Florodora and, although she doesn't know it, the whole concern is rightfully hers. Gilfain has a daughter of his own, Angela, whom he wishes to marry his manager, Frank Abercoed, for the latter has just inherited a title. But Angela loves a Captain Arthur Donegal, and Frank and Dolores love one another. A phrenologist, Anthony Tweedlepunch, assures Frank and Dolores that their cranial 'bumps' make it plain that they are exactly the right partners for Angela and Gilfain respectively. They prefer to disregard this, and Frank leaves the island to make arrangements for Dolores to join him.

When, subsequently, Gilfain learns that Dolores has gone to Britain, he buys a castle in Wales and installs himself there with Angela, his companion from Florodora,

Lady Holyrood, and a host of other beauties. Frank Abercoed gains admission to the castle dressed as an old harpist, while Dolores and Tweedlepunch, who has discovered the deception being practised on her and helped her to leave Florodora, arrive disguised as wandering musicians. The three contrive some apparently super-natural manifestations which convince Gilfain that he is being haunted by the castle's former owner. In his terror he confesses that Florodora belongs to Dolores. She and Frank are able to marry, Angela is permitted to accept Captain Donegal, and Gilfain consoles himself with Lady Holyrood.

PRINCIPAL NUMBERS

Act 1 'The credit's due to me' (Florodorians)
'The silver star of love' (Dolores)
'When I leave town' (Lady Holyrood)
'Galloping' (Angela and Donegal)
'I want to marry a man, I do' (Lady Holyrood, Tweedlepunch and Gilfain)
'The fellow who might' (Angela and chorus)
'Phrenology' (Tweedlepunch)
'What an interfering person' (Lady Holyrood, Donegal and Angela)
'The shade of the palm' ('Oh, my Dolores') (Frank)
Act 2 'Tact' (Lady Holyrood)
'The millionaire' (Gilfain and chorus)
'Tell me, pretty maiden, are there any more at home like you?' (Girls and Gilfain's clerks)
'I've an inkling' (Lady Holyrood)
'The Queen of the Philippine Islands' (Dolores)
'I want to be a military man' (Donegal)
'Willie was a gay boy' (Angela)

52

Flower-drum Song, *a musical play in two acts. Music by Richard Rodgers, lyrics by Oscar Hammerstein II, book by Oscar Hammerstein II and Joseph Fields. First produced: New York, 1958; London, 1960. Set in San Francisco's Chinatown in contemporary period.* (Performing rights: Williamson Music Limited.)

Sammy Fong, a thoroughly Americanized Chinese, wishes to arrange a marriage between Mei Li, a shy, demure girl, newly arrived in the United States, and Wang Ta, elder son of the prosperous Wang Chi Yang. The boy's father approves very much of the girl; but her father, Doctor Li, is against the match, while Wang Ta, for his part, is already in love with Linda Low, proprietress of a nightclub, who is far more ebullient and sexually assertive than Mei Li. However, Wang Chi Yang's wishes prevail, and preparations begin for the wedding.

Sammy, who has been contracted to marry Mei Li himself, but really wants Linda, is gratified at the way things are developing, but his pleasure evaporates when Wang Ta seems determined to marry her, despite his father. Sammy arranges for that respectable old gentleman to see Linda's act in her club, which culminates in a strip-tease. Wang Chi Yang is shocked and vows to prevent his son marrying such a girl. However, it is his son himself who is soon confessing his disillusionment with Linda and submitting to marriage with Mei Li. The only complication now is that Mei Li will not have him, believing mistakenly that a night he had passed in the flat of a woman friend, Helen Chai, had not been spent platonically.

53

Sammy Fong delightedly declares his intention of marrying Linda. He is thwarted by the Three Family Association, to whom the whole matter has been submitted for arbitration. They decree that Sammy must marry Mei Li. It is left until the very moment of the wedding ceremony for Mei Li to resolve everything by admitting that she had entered the United States as an illegal immigrant, which nullifies her contractual obligations, renders the Three Family Association powerless to dictate to her, and sets her free to marry Wang Ta.

PRINCIPAL NUMBERS

Act 1   'You are beautiful' (Wang Ta and Mme Liang)
'A hundred million miracles' (Mei Li, Doctor Li, Mme Liang, Wang Chi Yang, Liu Ma)
'I enjoy being a girl' (Linda)
'I am going to like it here' (Mei Li)
'Like a god' (Wang Ta)
'Chop Suey' (Mme Liang, Wang Sam and guests)
'Don't marry me' (Sammy Fong and Mei Li)
'Grant Avenue' (Linda and ensemble)
'Love look away' (Helen)

Act 2   Wang Ta's Dream Ballet
'The other generation' (Mme Liang and Wang Chi Yang)
'Sunday' (Linda and Sammy Fong)

The Geisha, *a musical play in two acts. Music by Sidney Jones, book by Owen Hall, lyrics by Harry Greenbank. First produced: London, 1896. Set in Japan in contemporary period.* (Performing rights: Emile Littler Musical Plays.)

Among the Royal Navy officers from H.M.S. *Turtle* who regularly frequent the Tea-house of Ten Thousand Joys, run by a Chinaman, Wun-hi, is Lieutenant Reginald Fairfax. His principal pleasure there is not the tea, but the most beautiful of the Geishas, O Mimosa San. The fact that he is engaged to Molly Seamore, a hearty member of the English colony, and that O Mimosa San has a Japanese fiancé, Lieutenant Katana, deters neither of them.

Also unperturbed by Katana's claims is the Provincial Governor, the Marquis Imari. Finding Mimosa with Reginald, he informs Wun-hi that he intends to marry Mimosa himself the following day. Sensing a fall in trade if his most popular Geisha is taken away, Wun-hi begs Juliette, his French interpreter, to deflect the Governor's interest towards herself, which she is only too willing to do. Unfortunately, Imari again finds Reginald and Mimosa together, and when the British officer insults him he orders the closure of the tea-house and the auctioning off of the girls.

Mimosa knows that Imari will buy her at the auction. Luckily, Molly Seamore, who has heard that her Reginald has become attracted by some Japanese girl or other, appeals to Mimosa for advice. Mimosa persuades Molly that if she makes herself look Japanese it will probably attract Reginald back to her: Mimosa's real hope is that Imari will fall for Molly instead of her.

Molly duly appears at the auction in full Japanese guise, and Imari is duly interested. This does not suit Juliette, who has already pictured herself as the Governor's Lady, but he bids for Molly and wins her. This places Molly in a quandary, for she wanted Reginald, not Imari. It is Mimosa and Juliette who resolve everything with an ingenious scheme whereby Juliette is willingly substituted for Molly at Imari's wedding ceremony and married to him. Reginald has by now come round to loving Molly again, Mimosa goes back to her Lieutenant Katana, and Wun-hi happily resumes business.

PRINCIPAL NUMBERS

Act 1   'Jack's the boy' (Reginald and officers)
         'That dear little Jappy Jap Jappy' (Cunningham)
         'The amorous goldfish' (Mimosa)
         'We're going to call on the Marquis' (Reginald and
            officers)
         'The toy' (Molly and Reginald)
         'A Geisha's life' (Mimosa)
         'Jack's the Boy' (Reginald and officers)
Act 2   'The toy monkey' (Molly)
         'Ching-a-ring-a-ree' (Juliette and Wun-hi)
         'The jewel of Asia' (Mimosa)
         'Star of my soul' (Reginald)
         'Chin Chin Chinaman' (Wun-hi and chorus)
         'The interfering parrot' (Molly)

Girl Crazy, *a musical comedy in two acts. Music by George Gershwin, book by Guy Bolton and John McGowan, lyrics by Ira Gershwin. First produced: New York, 1930. Set in Arizona and New Mexico in contemporary period.* (Performing rights: Macdonald & Young.)

The story is thin, but the wit of the lyrics and the effectiveness of the music have made some of its numbers enduringly familiar. All that matters about the plot is that the playboy Danny Churchill is 'banished' from New York by his wealthy father, who wants him to mend his ways. He travels the long distance to Custerville, Arizona, in the taxicab of a lively character, Gieber Goldfarb, and conceives the notion that if he is to be thus separated from the fleshly and bibulous delights of Manhattan he will recreate them for himself in the little Western town. He imports Broadway boys and girls to staff the dude ranch and gambling rooms he opens, and places them under the supervision of a man named Slick Fothergill and his strident, uninhibited wife, Kate.

Most of the show's content emanates from these characters and their relationships. As for Danny, he is introduced to simple values by the town's attractive postmistress, Molly Gray. The well-known number 'Bidin' my time', attributed below to 'The Foursome', belongs to a rustic male quartet who sing it repeatedly as a kind of punctuation to the staging.

Act 1 'The lonesome cowboy' (The Foursome and cowboys)

'Bidin' my time' (The Foursome)

'Could you use me?' (Danny and Molly)

'Bronco busters' (Dudeens and cowboys)

'Barbary Coast' (Patsy, Tess and ensemble)

'Embraceable you' (Danny and Molly)

'Finaletto' (Gieber, Slick and chorus)

'Sam and Delilah' (Kate and ensemble)

'I got rhythm' (Kate and The Foursome)

Act 2 'Land of the gay caballero' (Chorus)

'But not for me' (Molly and Gieber)

'Treat me rough' (Slick, girls and dancers)

'Boy! What love has done to me' (Kate)

'When it's cactus time in Arizona' (Molly and cowboys)

The Girl Friend, *a musical comedy in two acts. Music and lyrics by Con Conrad, Gus Kahn, Richard Rodgers and Lorenz Hart, book by R. P. Weston and Bert Lee, based on* Kitty's Kisses *by P. Bartholomae and Otto Harbach. First produced: New York, 1926; London, 1927. Set in the Canadian Rocky Mountains and the Hotel Wendell in contemporary period.* (Performing rights: Macdonald & Young.)

A railway train comes to a halt during its long journey through the Rocky Mountains and leaves again without one of its passengers, Robert Mason, who has become attracted by a fellow passenger, Kitty Brown, and has got off the train to look for her missing handbag. Kitty remains aboard and reaches the Hotel Wendell, where she is to meet her mother. Her mother has not turned up, and Kitty is unable to convince the cynical receptionist, Jerry, that she has lost her handbag and really will be able to pay her bill in due course. On the point of being turned away from the hotel she is rescued by its pert telephone operator, Jennie, who tells her that one of the two rooms of the bridal suite is vacant. The Mrs Dennison who should be in it has walked out on her husband, Richard, because of a suspected association between him and a blonde. Kitty does as Jennie suggests: pretends to be Mrs Dennison and occupies the vacant bedroom.

A mix-up as to which of the two bedrooms a breakfast tray is intended for introduces Richard and Kitty to one another for the first time next morning. Mrs Dennison's unexpected return, to find her husband seemingly involved with yet another girl, bring things to crisis point. She summons her lawyer: he proves to be none less than Kitty's admirer from the train, Robert Mason, who, in the circumstances, is only too happy to act for Mrs Dennison. It is left to the intervention of Jerry and Jennie to resolve things happily for everyone.

PRINCIPAL NUMBERS

Act 1 'Step on the track' (College boys and girls, and porters)
'Blue room' (Kitty and Robert)
'Boys of Hagerstown' (College boys and girls)
'What's the use of talking?' (Miss Wendell, Philip and chorus)
'The girl friend' (Jennie, Jerry and chorus)
'Boo-boo-boodledum' ('We must discover that girl') (Robert, Richard and Philip)

Glamorous Night, *a romantic play with music in three acts by Ivor Novello, with lyrics by Christopher Hassall. First produced: London, 1935. Set in an imaginary Balkan kingdom in contemporary period.* (Performing rights: Samuel French Ltd.)

Krasnia is nominally ruled by King Stefan VIII, but the potent influence behind the throne is his mistress, the fiery, Romany-born prima donna of the State Opera, Militza Hajos. The Prime Minister, Baron Lydyeff, who is also the leader of a growing revolutionary movement, has no doubt that if Militza could be removed from the scene the King would soon consent to abdicate. To this end, an assassination attempt upon the singer is made. As she and the tenor Lorenti are concluding their last duet in the première performance of a new operetta, *Glamorous Night*, a man runs towards the stage brandishing a pistol. Only the quick action of a young man in a stalls seat spoils the would-be assassin's aim and saves Militza's life.

Next morning her saviour is brought to her grand residence to be thanked. He proves to be an Englishman named Anthony Allen, visiting Krasnia in the course of a world cruise while trying to raise finance to develop his invention of a television system. Militza contributes a thousand pounds towards his needs and he leaves to return to the cruise liner *Silver Star*.

A less agreeable visitor follows: Prime Minister Lydyeff, bearing Militza's passport with orders from the King that she is to leave the country without delay, and never return. Lydyeff's revolutionary mobs are already roaming the streets, and King Stefan has yielded to an ultimatum. After a futile show of defiance, Militza leaves with her maid Phoebe to board the *Silver Star*, where, to her annoyance, she finds that the luxury suite she demands is already taken by an Englishman, who refuses to give it up. She demands to see him and discovers that he is Anthony Allen.

A ship's concert is enlivened by the singing of 'Shanty Town' by a coloured girl stowaway, Cleo Wellington, and followed by a song by Militza from *Glamorous Night*. Anthony Allen has become suspicious of a nefarious-looking passenger who frequently visits the ship's engine-room, and arranges for Militza and himself to be put ashore. Before this can be done a tremendous explosion occurs and the liner begins to sink. Baron Lydyeff, it seems, has struck at Militza once more, only to be foiled again, for she and Anthony reach the shore safely. They are by now in love and, encountering Militza's Romany people, are able to marry in a blood-ceremony.

In Krasnia, Lydyeff hands King Stefan an abdication document and gives him ten seconds to sign it, or be shot. The shot which rings out, however, is fired by Anthony Allen, and it is Lydyeff who falls dead. Militza's people have marched on Krasnia and defeated the revolutionaries. Ironically, this triumph ends Militza's and Anthony's romance. Realizing how the King depends on her guidance she accepts his invitation to share his throne, while Anthony ruefully departs with all the money he needs to complete his television system, promising that his lost beloved shall be the first person to appear on his screens.

PRINCIPAL NUMBERS

Act 1   'Her Majesty Militza' (Chorus)
'Shine through my dreams and once again' (Lorenti)
'Fold your wings of love around me' (Militza and Lorenti)
'Glamorous Night' ('Deep in my heart') (Militza)
Operetta (Chorus and Ballet)

Act 2   'When the gypsy played' (Militza)
Rumba
Skating Waltz
'Shanty Town' (Cleo)

Act 3   'The Gypsy Wedding' (Militza, Anthony and ensemble)
'Krasnian National Anthem' (Chorus)
'Singing Waltz' (Chorus)

A Greek Slave, *a musical comedy in two acts. Music by Sidney Jones, libretto by Owen Hall, lyrics by Harry Green-bank and Adrian Ross. First produced: London, 1898. Set in ancient Rome. (Performing rights: Emile Littler Musical Plays.)*

A Persian soothsayer, Heliodorus, and his daughter Maia, are conducting a thriving business at their villa in Rome, where the nobility come to learn their fortunes. Much of Heliodorus's information is derived from the gossipy Iris, maid to the Princess Antonia, and is therefore remarkably accurate.

The Princess is loved by the Prefect of Rome, Marcus Pomponius, but has never herself felt the pangs of love. Hearing that she is on her way to consult Heliodorus, the Prefect gets there first and tells the soothsayer his requirements. Maia suggests that the first thing to do is to get Antonia to learn to love, then manipulate her affections towards the Prefect afterwards. Heliodorus's talented Greek slave, Archias, who is in love with Iris, has been sculpting a statue of Eros, using his fellow slave Diomed as model. It is proposed to excite Antonia's passions by showing her this statue; but when she arrives Diomed has taken the statue's place, and it is him she bears away, leaving Maia, who loves him, to reflect that her plan has succeeded but has left her with a statue instead of a lover.

Diomed's performance at the Princess Antonia's villa is less than impressive, and she has to make most of the amorous advances herself; but at least she has learnt to love. After numerous complications of mistaken identity as the Prefect tries to further his suit, the various slaves are reunited with their respective loves and saturnalian revels prevail.

PRINCIPAL NUMBERS

Act 1   'The wizard' (Heliodorus)
         'Confidential' (Iris)
         'Freedom' (Diomed)
         'We are noble Roman ladies' (Lucinea, Flavia, Tullia and Cornelia)
         'The lost Pleiad' (Maia)
         'I cannot love' (Antonia)
         'Invocation' (Maia)

Act 2 'A song of love' (Antonia)
'Oh, what will be the end of it?' (Iris and Heliodorus)
'The golden isle' (Maia)
'I want to be popular' (Marcus and chorus)
'The girl of my heart' (Diomed and chorus)
'I'm a naughty girl: A frog he lived in a pond' (Iris and chorus)
'Nothing but nerves' (Heliodorus)

Guys and Dolls, *a musical in two acts. Music and lyrics by Frank Loesser, book by Jo Swerling and Abe Burrows, based on a story and characters by Damon Runyon. First produced: New York, 1950; London, 1953. Set in New York and Havana in the early 1930s.* (Performing rights: Edwin H. Morris & Co. Limited.)

The Salvation Army's Save-a-Soul Mission on New York's Broadway, run by Arvide Abernathy, is not doing too well. There are plenty of souls about, but most of them are too preoccupied with gambling or entertaining or being entertained to care about being saved.

One who comes into this uninhibited category is Sky Masterson, a lady-killer who chances to meet one of the Salvation Army lasses, Sarah Brown, and finds her attractive enough to make him think it worthwhile devoting some of his valuable time to pursuing her. He prospers to the extent of persuading her to go to Havana with him, albeit reluctantly. While they are there she realizes she has fallen in love with him, but when they return to New

1. *The Belle of New York*. Edna May as Violet Gray, leads The Ornamental Purity Brigade. Shaftesbury Theatre, 1898.

2. *The Arcadians*. Ada Blanche as Mrs Smith, Dan Rolyat as James Smith, rejuvenated as Simplicitas, and Akerman May as Sir George Paddock. Shaftesbury Theatre, 1909.

3. *The Quaker Girl*. Gertie Millar as Prudence and Joseph Coyne as
Tony Chute. Adelphi Theatre, 1910.

4. *Chu Chin Chow*. Oscar Asche as Abu Hasan alias Chu Chin Chow. His Majesty's Theatre, 1916.

5. *The Maid of the Mountains*. José Collins as Teresa. Daly's Theatre, 1917.

6. *The Vagabond King*. Saved in the nick of time. Derek Oldham as François Villon. Winter Garden Theatre, 1927.

7. *Sally.* 'Look for the Silver Lining.' Dorothy Dickson as Sally and Leslie Henson as Constantine. Winter Garden Theatre, 1921.

8. *The Desert Song*. 'There is your pistol, and here is my heart!' Harry Welchman as Pierre Birabeau (the Red Shadow) and Edith Day as Margot Bonvalet. Theatre Royal, Drury Lane, 1927.

9. *Bitter-Sweet*. 'I'll see you again.' Peggy Wood as Sarah Millick and
George Metaxa as Carl Linden. His Majesty's Theatre, 1929.

10. *Show Boat*. Drama on the *Cotton Blossom*. Viola Compton as Parthy Ann Hawks, Edith Day as Magnolia, Dorothy Lena as Ellie, Marie Burke as Julie, Colin Clive as Steve, Cedric Hardwicke as Captain Andy, Jack Martin as Windy, Percy Parsons as Vallon, Alberta Hunter as Queenie and Paul Robeson as Joe. Theatre Royal, Drury Lane, 1928.

11. *Glamorous Night.* The gipsy wedding. Ivor Novello as Anthony Allen and Mary Ellis as Militza Hajos. Theatre Royal, Drury Lane, 1935.

12. *Annie Get Your Gun.* 'I'm an Indian too.' Dolores Gray as Annie Oakley. Coliseum, 1947.

13. *Oklahoma!* 'The Surrey with the Fringe on top.' Howard Keel as Curly and Betty Jane Watson as Laurey. Theatre Royal, Drury Lane, 1947.

14. *Kiss Me Kate*. 'We open in Venice.' Patricia Morison as Katharine, Bill Johnson as Petruchio, Julie Wilson as Bianca and Walter Long as Lucentio. Coliseum, 1951.

15. *The Sound of Music*. 'Do-Re-Me.' Jean Bayless as Maria Rainer with the children. Palace Theatre, 1961.

16. *The King and I.* 'Shall we dance?' Gertrude Lawrence as Anna Leonowens and Yul Brynner as the King. St James Theatre, New York, 1951.

York and she learns that some of his fellow-gamblers had bet him he would never succeed with her, she drops him.

Crisis-time has arrived for the Mission, which must close through sheer lack of business. It is Sky who, with his wide range of contacts, comes to the rescue, crowding the place out with souls cheerfully agreeing to be saved. Sarah takes him back; and the love-exasperation relationship of a nightclub entertainer, Adelaide, and a gambler, Nathan Detroit, which has been interweaving with theirs, is also settled in favour of love.

PRINCIPAL NUMBERS

Act 1 'Follow the fold' (Sarah, Arvide, Agatha and Mission group)
'I'll know' (Sarah and Sky)
'A bushel and a peck' (Adelaide and Hot-box Dolls)
'Adelaide's lament' (Adelaide)
'Guys and dolls' (Nicely and Benny)
'If I were a bell' (Sarah)
'My time of day' (Sky)
'I've never been in love before' (Sky and Sarah)
Act 2 'Take back your mink' (Adelaide and Dolls)
'Luck be a lady' (Sky and crap-shooters)
'Sue me' (Adelaide and Nathan)
'Sit down, you're rockin' the boat' (Nicely)
'Marry the man today' (Adelaide and Sarah)

Hit the Deck, *a musical comedy in two acts, adapted from the play* Shore Leave *by R. P. Weston and Bert Lee. Music by Vincent Youmans. First produced: New York, 1927; London, 1927. Set in Newport, Rhode Island, and at sea in contemporary period.* (Performing rights: Macdonald & Young.)

The plot of this show has little substance, and the events are mostly episodic, rather than cumulative. They concern the efforts of Looloo, the proprietress of a coffee shop in Newport, Rhode Island, to persuade one of the many sailors who patronize the establishment to marry her. Bill, as he is called, is attracted enough by her but is sensitive about his lowly position: Looloo has plenty of money while he has none, and his scruples will not allow him to gratify her wish.

Bill's ship is due to sail on a protracted cruise, so Looloo shuts her shop and contrives to get aboard. She continues her wooing wherever they go, but always in vain until she has the bright idea of renouncing her money in favour of their first-born child: a simple solution for a simple sailor, and it works.

PRINCIPAL NUMBERS

Act 1   'Join the Navy' (Chorus)
           'Jack and Jill' (Looloo and chorus)
           'A kiss or two' (Charlotte and girls)
           'Fancy me just meeting you' (Looloo and Bill)
           'Lucky bird' (Magnolia)
           'Looloo' (Looloo and sailors)
           'Nothing could be sweeter' (Charlotte and Mat)
           'Sometimes I'm happy' (Looloo and Bill)

Irene, *a musical comedy in two acts. Music by Harry Tierney, book by James Montgomery, lyrics by Joseph McCarthy. First produced: New York, 1919; London, 1920. Set in America in contemporary period.* (Performing rights: Macdonald & Young.)

Irene O'Dare works in the upholstery department of a large store, and when a complaint is received from a wealthy young man, Donald Marshall, about some material he has bought, she is sent to investigate. Donald questions her about her background and is touched to hear of her poor home and her longing for nice clothes and good society. He sees a way to help her. A male friend of his from London has recently set himself up in business in America as a modiste, under the name 'Madame Lucy'; but despite his great talents he has not yet made any mark. What is needed is for a few society girls to be seen wearing his creations, which will become talked about. Donald suggests that Irene leave her job and work for Madame Lucy in this way, which she proceeds to do, persuading two of her workmates, Helen and Jane, to join her.

Irene proves an immediate hit in society. One of the most enthusiastic of the many men who admire her is a wealthy social climber, J. P. Beaudon, who loses no time in proposing to her, backing up the offer with a string of pearls. When he learns the truth about her background he just as quickly retracts, and the way is left clear for Donald, whom Irene has loved all along, to produce his pearls and proposal, which she gladly accepts.

Jill Darling, *a musical comedy in two acts. Music by Vivian Ellis, with additional numbers by Edward Horan, book by Marriott Edgar, additional lyrics and scenes by Desmond Carter and Conrad Carter. First produced: London, 1934. Set in England in contemporary period.* (Performing rights: Samuel French Ltd.)

Sir Timothy Bunting, of Bunting Hall, a rabid advocate of temperance, is happily anticipating the arrival of a Parliamentary candidate, Pendleton Brookes, whose chief platform is the temperance issue. Unfortunately, Brookes does not practise what he preaches, and reaches Bunting Hall helplessly intoxicated.

Unobtrusively present at the reception party is his cousin, Jack Crawford, son of Colonel Crawford, who runs the local country club, The Double Six. Disapproving of Bunting as much as the latter does of him, the Colonel has forbidden any of his family to visit Bunting Hall; but Jack has gone there, disguised as a waiter, to watch his estranged actress girl friend, Jill Sonning, entertain the company with her cabaret. Jack and Jill are reconciled and when Brookes proves incapable of delivering his speech, Jack, who resembles him, manages to take his place successfully, but comes adrift when he is given a glass of Bunting's non-alcoholic drink, 'Ososober': he finds it revolting and calls for beer. In the midst of the uproar he is arrested by police in mistake for Brookes, who is wanted for dangerous driving. Jill, Jack's sister April, and her fiancé, Bobby Jones, try to rescue him from the police station, which results in their own arrest. All escape, thanks to an ingenious plan, and the ending is rendered doubly happy for everyone by Bunting's decision to turn his temperance-drink factory into a brewery.

PRINCIPAL NUMBERS

Act 1   'The Nineteenth hole' (Jack and men)
      'Budapest' (Jill and chorus)
      'Let's lay our heads together' (Jack and Jill)
      'A flower for you' (Jill)
      'Czardas' (Jill and chorus)
      'Nonny-nonny-no' (April and Bobby)
Act 2   'I'm on a see-saw' (April and Bobby)
      'Bats in the belfry' (Jean and chorus)

The King and I, *a musical in two acts. Music by Richard Rodgers, book and lyrics by Oscar Hammerstein II, based on the novel* Anna and the King of Siam *by Margaret Landon. First produced: New York, 1951; London, 1953. Set in Siam in the 1860s.* (Performing rights: Williamson Music Limited.)

The King is the King of Siam, and 'I' is Anna Leonowens, a widowed but still young and attractive English school-teacher, whom he has engaged to come to his country and instil Western culture into his dozens of princes and princesses. She is not pleased to find that she is expected to live in the palace on the level of a servant, rather than in a house of her own, with her son Louis, and she is not impressed to see a Burmese girl, Tuptim, brought as a 'present' to the King, escorted by one of her countrymen, Lun Tha. But although Anna and the stubborn King find themselves at loggerheads, she quickly achieves rapport with the princes and princesses.

   She also learns to appreciate the King's difficulties in overcoming his inbred feudalism, and springs hotly to his defence when news arrives that the British Government is sending a Commissioner to find out whether reports of barbaric conditions in Siam are true, and, if so, to annexe the country. She suggests that the King entertain the Commissioner with a grand reception, at which all his family will be dressed in European style and a ballet she will arrange for them will be presented, as proof of the country's cultural development. This works beautifully and the Commissioner goes away much impressed. But Anna's opinion of the King is promptly lowered when he discovers that Tuptim and Lun Tha are in love, and the

latter is killed and the former ordered to be flogged. Anna
manages to get the girl reprieved, but she feels she can
remain in Siam no longer. Before she can leave, though,
the King becomes mortally ill, and she consents to his
deathbed wish that she will remain and continue her good
work for his country.

PRINCIPAL NUMBERS

Act 1 'I whistle a happy tune' (Anna and Louis)
      'My lord and master' (Tuptim)
      'Hello, young lovers' (Anna)
      'A puzzlement' (King)
      'Getting to know you' (Anna, King's wives and
          children)
      'We kiss in the shadow' (Tuptim and Lun Tha)
      'Shall I tell you what I think of you'? (Anna)
      'Something wonderful' (Lady Thiang)
Act 2 'Western people funny' (Lady Thiang and King's
          wives)
      'I have dreamed' (Tuptim and Lun Tha)
      Ballet: The small house of Uncle Thomas
      'The King's Song' (King)
      'Shall we dance?' (Anna and King)

King's Rhapsody, *a musical romance in three acts. Music
and book by Ivor Novello, lyrics by Christopher Hassall. First
produced: London, 1949. Set in two Northern kingdoms and
Paris, early in the 20th century.* (Performing rights:
Samuel French Ltd.)

Unlike the victims of most arranged marriages in stage

works, Princess Cristiane of Norseland is eagerly looking forward to hers with Nikki, heir to the throne of Murania, whose father has just died. Since childhood she has been filling scrapbooks with pictures of the handsome prince. Nikki proves less than thrilled, but resigns himself to his fate, assuring his mistress, Marta Karillos, that though he is duty bound to marry and beget an official heir, she will always be his real love.

Cristiane and her companion, Countess Vera Lemmkainen, arrive in the Muranian capital, to find Nikki absent, ostensibly on military duties. When he arrives, a week later, he finds his Queen-to-be in her boudoir, playing the piano, and in his slightly tipsy state believes her to be her maid. At any rate, he finds her enchanting and they are soon closing the curtains on the gipsy serenaders outside.

Later, at a ball, Nikki is humiliated to learn Cristiane's true identity and pointedly dances with Marta Karillos instead of her. Nevertheless, he has to go through with the marriage, and nine months later their first child is due to be born: Nikki prefers to spend the evening with his mistress. Six weeks later, with her son safely born, Cristiane demands that Nikki expel Marta, at which he threatens to leave as well. Marta is suddenly brought in, having been attacked by a mob for causing unhappiness to the Queen. Cristiane tells the crowd that Marta is her friend, and they disperse. This unselfish act convinces Nikki finally of Cristiane's love for him.

Nikki and Marta are not finished for ever, though. When Nikki tries to democratize his country, he is forced to abdicate and go into exile without Cristiane. Ten years after, when Cristiane's son is about to be crowned the new King of Murania, Nikki is with Marta at a Paris opera when his country's Prime Minister arrives to invite him to the Coronation. He will not promise; but after the ceremony in his ex-capital's cathedral the deposed King steps from the shadows, picks up a rose Cristiane has dropped, and kneels to pray for the young King, his son.

PRINCIPAL NUMBERS

Act 1   'Some day my heart will awake' (Cristiane)
        'The National Anthem of Murania' (Chorus)
        'Fly home, little heart' (Vera)
        'Mountain dove' (Cristiane)
        'If this were love' (Cristiane)
Act 2   'The Mayor of Perpignon' (Marta and chorus)
        'The gates of Paradise' (Cristiane, Vera and Egon)
Act 3   'Take your girl' (Vera and chorus)
        'The violin began to play' (Cristiane)
        Muranian Rhapsody (Ballet and chorus)
        Coronation scene: *O Ev themonis Petheon*

Kiss Me Kate, *a musical in two acts. Music and lyrics by Cole Porter, book by Sam and Bella Spewack. First produced: New York, 1948; London, 1951. Set in Baltimore, Maryland, in contemporary period.* (Performing rights: Evans Plays.)

A reconciliation seems to be within sight for Fred Graham and Lilli Vanessi, members of a theatrical company presenting a musical version of Shakespeare's *The Taming of the Shrew.* They had been married, though subsequently divorced; but each is now realizing that they belong together again. A gift of flowers, intended by Fred for the female lead,

73

Lois, but delivered to Lilli by mistake, confirms her in this belief. When Lilli finds out at length that the bouquet was not meant for her after all, she announces that she will leave the company at once.

She is prevented from doing so by the arrival of gangsters, come to put pressure on another member of the company, Bill Calhoun, who owes a $10,000 gambling debt. He is saved by the outcome of an underworld power struggle, which ousts his creditors from control and nullifies his debt. His girl friend, Lois, forgives him for his compulsive gambling, and Lilli and Fred now decide to remarry.

This contemporary story is played out in parallel with scenes from *The Taming of the Shrew*, some of whose situations resemble those in which the actors find themselves in 'real life'. Lilli and Fred play the leading roles of Katharine and Petruchio; Lois and Bill are Bianca and Lucentio.

PRINCIPAL NUMBERS

Act 1 'Another op'nin', another show' (Hattie and chorus)

'Why can't you behave?' (Lois)

'*Wunderbar*' (Lilli and Fred)

'So in love' (Lilli)

'We open in Venice' (Katharine, Petruchio, Bianca, Lucentio and chorus)

'Tom, Dick or Harry' (Bianca and suitors)

'I've come to wive it wealthily in Padua' (Petruchio and chorus)

'I hate men' (Katharine)

'Were thine that special face' (Petruchio)

'I sing of love' (Bianca, Lucentio and chorus)

74

Lady Be Good, *a musical comedy in two acts. Music by George Gershwin, lyrics by Ira Gershwin, book by Guy Bolton and Fred Thompson. First produced: New York, 1924; London, 1926. Set in America in contemporary period.* (Performing rights: Macdonald & Young.)

Dick and Susie Trevor are a brother and sister in the vaudeville business – a song-and-dance act. Engagements are becoming fewer and further between and they are at the end of their money when the personable and still cheerful Dick meets a rich girl who promptly falls in love with him. Had he been aware that she is the owner of the lodgings which he and Susie share, perhaps he would have been a little more discreet in letting her see that her interest is not reciprocated. As it is, he makes it all too plain, and she takes revenge for the rebuff by having the couple evicted, with no alternative but to set up home in the street.

Dick decides that he will have to respond to the rich girl's advances after all, but Susie comes to the rescue and manages to save him, just in time for their fortunes to change.

Act 1 'Nice work if you can get it' (Dick and chorus)
'Hang on to me' (Dick and Susie)
'I've got a crush on you' (Bertie and Daisy)
'Fascinating rhythm' (Susie, Dick and chorus)
'I've got a feeling I'm falling' (Jack)
'So am I' (Jack and Susie)
'Lady be good' (Watty, Bertie and chorus)

Act 2 'Linger in the lobby' (Parke and chorus)
'I'd rather Charleston' (Susie and Dick)
'The half of it, dearie blues' (Shirley and Dick)
'Juanita' (Parke and chorus)
'Love walked in' (Jack)
'Swiss Miss' (Susie)

The Lisbon Story, *a play with music in two acts. Music by Harry Parr Davies, book and lyrics by Harold Purcell. First produced: London, 1943. Set in Paris and Lisbon in 1938–42.* (Performing rights: Chappell & Co. Ltd.)

Just before the war a Parisian singing star, Gabrielle Girard, parts from the man she loves, David Warren, of the British Foreign Office, who has been posted to Washington. They chance to meet again in that neutral centre of wartime intrigue, Lisbon, where David and an Irishman, Mike O'Rourke, are caring for a girl named Lisette Sargon, whose father, a scientist with important secrets for the Allies, is expected to be smuggled from France to join her. Gabrielle takes the girl into her home; but her father's arrival under cover of Carnival time does not happen. He has been imprisoned by the Nazis in France, although his identity is not known.

Gabrielle has a keen German follower, Karl von Schriner, a cultural representative whose job is to persuade distinguished artists from occupied countries to return home and resume their careers, to raise the people's morale. Gabrielle has declined his overtures – both professional and romantic – so far, but now she agrees to go back to Paris if he will let her choose the people to appear with her and run her theatre. He agrees, and by this means she is able to get Sargon released from concentration camp and reunites him with Lisette. But von Schriner has discovered the scientist's identity: he tells Gabrielle that if she will not become his mistress he will disclose all he knows.

David and Mike have a plan to smuggle Gabrielle, Sargon and Lisette to London immediately after the opening of her musical *La Comtesse*, in which Lisette has a part. Seeing von Schriner watching from the wings, and knowing they cannot all get away, Gabrielle ensures that Lisette and her father escape, at the cost of her own life from von Schriner's revolver.

PRINCIPAL NUMBERS

Act 1 'Happy days' (Panache)
'Some day we shall meet again' (Gabrielle)
'Never say goodbye' (Gonzalez and Gabrielle)
'Pedro the fisherman' (Fishermen and girls)
'Carnival song' (Carmelita)

Act 2 'Serenade for sale' (Ramon)
Finale of Act 1 of *La Comtesse* (Ensemble)
'April in the spring of love' (Lisette)
Finale of Act 2 of *La Comtesse*, and 'The Marseillaise'

77

The Maid of the Mountains, *a musical play in three acts. Music by Harold Fraser-Simson, with additional numbers by James W. Tate, book by Frederick Lonsdale, lyrics by Harry Graham, with additional lyrics by F. Clifford Harris and Valentine. First produced: Manchester, 1916; London, 1917. Revised versions by Emile Littler, 1942 and 1972. Set in a Latin country earlier this century.* (Performing rights: Emile Littler Musical Plays.)

Like W. S. Gilbert's Ruth in *The Pirates of Penzance*, Teresa is a sort of 'piratical maid of all-work' to the gang of mountain brigands led by Baldasarre. Baldasarre had once had a keen interest in her personal qualities, but this has waned, along with his enthusiasm for banditry. Finding his hideout surrounded by forces of law and order he prepares to disband the gang and sends the reluctant Maid of the Mountains to the safety of a nearby village. From a chance encounter with Vittoria, the daughter of General Malona, the retiring Governor of Santo, and her companion Angela, Baldasarre learns that the new Governor, who is unknown by sight in the town, will shortly pass by in his coach. News is brought that Teresa has been captured and will only be freed if Baldasarre gives himself up. He determines instead to waylay the coach and take the Governor's place.

This is successfully accomplished, and Baldasarre and his lieutenants, Beppo, Antonio and Carlo, dressed as the Governor and his staff, enter Santo in triumph. Baldasarre interviews Teresa and gives out that she has promised to betray the local brigands to him, quietly instructing her to stand by to join him and the others in a feigned expedition against the brigands, during which they will escape to safety. Unfortunately Baldasarre has become attracted to Angela and puts off the move. Teresa recognizes the reason and reveals the impostors' true identities. They are arrested and sentenced to be deported to Devil's Island.

The garrison of Devil's Island is commanded by a Lieutenant Rugini, who has been posted there to cool his ardour for Angela. It has been discovered that Antonio is the husband of Vittoria, the daughter of the former Governor of Santo, but had been believed lost at sea some years before. Visiting Devil's Island with her father, Vittoria tries to bribe Rugini to let Antonio escape, but he refuses. Teresa, who has been pardoned for betraying her former comrades, tries to charm General Malona into letting her have Baldasarre; but the latter is more interested in Angela, and confesses as much to Rugini. The officer assures him that Teresa is worth far more than Angela, but Baldasarre will not listen. Rugini proceeds to prove his point: he organizes the escape of them all, himself included. When Teresa urges Baldasarre to go and join Angela, the unselfish gesture at last brings home to him the proof of her true love.

PRINCIPAL NUMBERS

Act 1   'Live for today' (Beppo)
      'My life is love' (Teresa)
      'Farewell' (Teresa)
Act 2   'Love will find a way' (Teresa)
      'Save us' (Chorus)
      'Dirty work' (General Malona and Antonio)
      'A paradise for two' (Teresa and Beppo)
      'Husbands and wives' (Vittoria and Antonio)
      'A bachelor gay' (Beppo)

79

Me and My Girl, *a musical comedy in two acts. Music by Noel Gay, book and lyrics by L. Arthur Rose and Douglas Furber. First produced: London, 1937. Set in England in contemporary period.* (Performing rights: Samuel French Ltd.)

The Earl of Hareford has died, and his estate and title have been awaiting his unknown heir. The latter has been discovered at last in the person of Bill Snibson, a barrow-boy in the London district of Lambeth. The Hareford family solicitor, Mr Parchester, produces him for inspection by the Duchess of Dene and Sir John Tremayne. Sir John's verdict is that a person from such a walk of life is quite unfitted to assume the earldom – to the evident relief of other relatives who had comfortably anticipated legacies in the absence of an heir. But the Duchess, for all that she is a martinet, sees Bill as suitable material for moulding and for marrying off to the beautiful Jacqueline Carson.

Bill is a personable young fellow, and Jacqueline enthusiastically plays her part in the moulding process, but neither she nor the Duchess can persuade him to give up his Lambeth sweetheart, Sally. Sally sees things more realistically, though, and, knowing herself unfitted to be a Countess, tries to precipitate a break by bringing a party of costers and their donahs to Bill's coming-out party at Hareford. She hopes their noisy, spirited 'Lambeth Walk' will make Bill see the difference between them and the well-bred people with whom he now mingles. Quite the opposite happens, with everyone – the Duchess included – joining in the infectious dance.

All the same, the Duchess decrees that Sally must go, and the humiliated girl leaves. She is sought out by an unexpected sympathizer, Sir John Tremayne, who knows what it is to suffer a shattered romance. In secret he coaches Sally, just as Bill is being coached, and the two are eventually reunited, as proper an Earl and Countess as could be imagined.

PRINCIPAL NUMBERS

Act 1   'Thinking of no one but me' (Jacqueline, Gerald and chorus)
        'Me and my girl' (Bill and Sally)
        'The family solicitor' (Parchester and chorus)
        'A bright little girl like me' (Bill, Jacqueline and chorus)
        'If only you had cared for me' (Duchess and Sir John)
        'Once you lose your heart' (Sally and chorus)
        'The Lambeth Walk' (Bill, Sally and chorus)
Act 2   'Don't be silly, Sally' (Sally and chorus)
        'Song of Hareford' (Duchess and chorus)

Merrie England, *a comic opera in two acts. Music by Edward German, book and lyrics by Basil Hood. First produced: London, 1902. Set at Windsor in Elizabethan times.* (Performing rights: Chappell & Co. Ltd.)

Sir Walter Raleigh, Court favourite of Queen Elizabeth I of England, loves one of her ladies-in-waiting, Bessie

Throckmorton. Bessie has lost a letter from him, and is fearful lest it should fall into the hands of the Queen, who would not favour the association. Instead, it comes into the possession of Raleigh's rival, the Earl of Essex, who is given it by an artless girl, Jill-All-Alone, who is being persecuted by the local people on suspicion of witchcraft.

The Queen attends the revels. Long Tom, a forester who has defended Jill from her accusers, begs the Queen's protection for her; but Essex hands Elizabeth the letter that had been in Jill's keeping. Believing for a moment that the 'Bessie' addressed in it is herself, but then learning that it refers to one of her maids, the incensed Queen orders Bessie's imprisonment, Raleigh's banishment, and for Jill death by burning, as a witch.

Jill and Bessie are imprisoned in Windsor Castle. But Jill knows a secret passage to Herne's Oak in the forest, and leads Bessie out by it. The Queen also happens to be in the forest, paying an apothecary for a poison with which she intends to have Bessie put to death. But the forest is an even busier place this night, for Sir Walter Raleigh, disguised as a forester, is there to overhear. After the Queen has gone he seizes the apothecary, who turns out to be the Queen's Fool and throws in his lot with Raleigh.

Essex has also decided to help Raleigh and Bessie marry, since this would further deflect the Queen's favour from his rival to himself. The ghost of Herne the Hunter, a former keeper of Windsor Forest, is said to appear whenever England's monarch is liable to commit a crime, so Essex has Long Tom disguised as Herne and hidden in Herne's Oak. When the Queen arrives to watch a masque the ghostly figure appears. The Queen recognizes the warning, pardons Bessie, Jill and Raleigh, and offers the jubilant Essex her arm.

82

Act 1   'Oh, where the deer do lie' (Jill and chorus)
'That every Jack should have a Jill' (Raleigh and chorus)
'Love is meant to make us glad' (May Queen, Kate, Raleigh, Wilkins and Long Tom)
'She had a letter from her love' (Bessie)
'Who were the yeomen?' (Essex and chorus)
'God save Elizabeth' (Chorus)
'O peaceful England' (Elizabeth)
'When Neptune sat on his lonely throne' (Wilkins and chorus)

Act 2   'In England, merrie England' (Bessie, Jill, Big Ben, Long Tom)
'It is the merry month of May' (Jill and Raleigh)
'The Queen o' May is crowned today' (Chorus and dance)
'Dan Cupid hath a garden' (Raleigh)
'O who shall say that love is cruel?' (Bessie)
'Robin Hood's wedding' (Ensemble)

The Messenger Boy, *a musical play in two acts. Music by Ivan Caryll and Lionel Monckton, book by James T. Tanner and Alfred Murray, lyrics by Adrian Ross and Percy Greenbank. First produced: London, 1900. Set in England and Egypt in contemporary period.* (Performing rights: Emile Littler Musical Plays.)

Messenger boys were a relatively new institution in 1900, gradually replacing those older men, the District Messengers, who would carry a message a mile or halfway across the world and seldom fail to deliver it. Tommy Bang is such a boy, and the furthest-flung errand of his career is to El Barra, in Egypt, where he has to hand an envelope to the Governor, Lord Punchestown.

The sender of this missive is a London financier, Tudor Pyke, and his act is one of jealous spite. He wants to marry Lord Punchestown's stepdaughter Nora, but she prefers the attentions of a messenger of a higher order than Tommy Bang – a Queen's Messenger named Clive Radnor. Clive has little money, and to make things worse has guaranteed a bill of payment which he cannot meet. Pyke has managed to get the bill into his hands. He has also got hold of a series of dressmaking bills incurred by Lady Punchestown which she cannot meet, either. By threatening to send her bills to her husband, as evidence of her extravagance behind his back, Pyke gets Lady Punchestown to consent to his having Nora. Clive has still to be eliminated from the running, though. He is going to join Lord Punchestown in Egypt, and Pyke decides to wreck his career by sending the Governor the bill Clive has backed, thus branding him unreliable and unsuitable.

Tommy Bang is duly dispatched on this errand, with instructions not to let anything whatsoever deflect him from his duty. Only when he has gone does Pyke discover that he has enclosed Lady Punchestown's bills in the envelope instead of Clive's, and from this point the show concerns his varied attempts to stop Tommy from delivering the envelope, and Tommy's determined efforts to complete his mission.

Act 1 'Ask Papa' (Nora and Clive)
'The messenger boy' (Tommy and chorus)
'Aspirations' (Rosa and Tommy)
'The pretty petticoat' (Clive and chorus)
'In the wash' (Mrs Bang and chorus)
'Ask the advice of the Captain' (Concerted piece)
Act 2 'A perfectly peaceful person' (Clive)
'When the boys come home once more' (Nora and chorus)
'Maisie is a daisy' (Isabel and chorus)
'They're all after Pott' (Captain Pott and chorus)
'I'm a little Dutch maid' (Rosa and Tommy)
'Captivating London' (Rosa and chorus)
'When the boys come home once more' (Nora and chorus)

Miss Hook of Holland, *a 'Dutch musical incident' in two acts. Music and lyrics by Paul A. Rubens, book by Paul A. Rubens and Austen Hurgon. First produced: London, 1907. Set in Holland in contemporary period.* (Performing rights: Emile Littler Musical Plays.)

'Cream of the Sky' is the name of a liqueur which has made the Dutch distilling firm of Hook famous. The recipe had been discovered by the widowed Mr Hook's daughter, Sally, but almost on the eve of the celebrations planned to mark the anniversary of this great success the piece of paper bearing the formula has been lost.

The finder is one Simon Slinks, a ne'er-do-well who

knows that the officer commanding the local soldiery, Captain Paap, is in love with Sally, who will have nothing to do with him, for she loves his young bandmaster, Van Vuyt. Slinks is right in thinking that Paap will pay him for the formula, in order to be able to restore it to Mr Hook and win his support in his wooing.

Mr Hook's maid Mina is engaged to his foreman, Schnapps. The latter takes on Slinks as a worker at the distillery, thus enabling Slinks to do yet another profitable deal by selling the job to Van Vuyt, who wishes to be on hand during the celebrations and forestall any moves Captain Paap may make in Sally's direction. Paap arrives with the missing recipe, but before he can hand it over he hears that Mr Hook suspects that whoever has it stole it, and has ordered the immediate arrest of anyone claiming to have 'found' it. Paap hastily seals it in an envelope and gives it to a workman to hand to Mr Hook anonymously. The workman happens to be Van Vuyt.

The unwitting bandmaster gives Mr Hook the envelope and finds himself under arrest as soon as its contents are discovered. Captain Paap promises further disciplinary action against Van Vuyt, whom he has now recognized, for being present at the celebration party against orders. Sally, however, has found that Paap is becoming increasingly interested in another girl, Freda Voos. As compensation for his fickleness to her she demands that he forgive Van Vuyt, and having achieved this she persuades her father to let her marry the bandmaster.

Act 1 'Mr Hook started quite low down in life' (Schnapps and chorus)

'We are little orphans' (Orphans)

'We've purchased our meat for dinner' (Chorus)

'We're soldiers of the Netherlands' (Paap and chorus)

'The Flying Dutchman' (Mina and chorus)

'Is there another man so envied in the land?' (Van Vuyt and chorus)

Act 2 Madrigal: 'Bottles'

'Little Miss Wooden Shoes' (Sally and girls)

'I've a little pink petty from Peter' (Mina)

'The house that Hook built' (Chorus)

'Harwich to Hook' (Schnapps and chorus)

'Cream of the Sky' (Sally)

The Mountebanks, *a comic opera in two acts. Music by Alfred Cellier, book and lyrics by W. S. Gilbert. First produced: London, 1892. Set in Sicily in the early 19th century.* (Performing rights: Chappell & Co. Ltd.)

During his collaboration with Arthur Sullivan, W. S. Gilbert often urged the merits of a magic 'lozenge', by which a whole community might be drugged into illusion. Sullivan resolutely resisted the idea, except in *The Sorcerer,* where drugged tea acts as a mass love potion. After their partnership ended Gilbert devised the plot of *The Mountebanks,* with its reliance upon a remarkable potion. Ironically, the piece reached the stage in the year following Sullivan's death.

Arrostino and his Sicilian brigands plan to take over a monastery and, disguised as the monks, to lure the passing Duke and Duchess of Pallavicini into their hands. A girl, Minestra, is to impersonate an old woman in distress and get the ducal coach to stop.

Alfredo, a peasant, exasperated by the whims of his girl Teresa, transfers his attentions to another girl, Ultrice. The landlord of the inn where the Duke and Duchess are to stay a night persuades the couple to impersonate them, in order that he may rehearse his welcome. Meanwhile, three mountebanks arrive in the village: Bartolo and Nita, who are in love, and their manager Pietro. The stars of the show, a pair of life-size clockwork dolls, have been delayed en route, so Bartolo and Nita agree to pretend to be them.

A dreadful explosion occurs. The victim is an old Alchemist, who has been staying at the inn, the only remaining trace of whom is a bottle of physic, whose label indicates that the drinker will become whatever he is pretending to be. Pietro gets Bartolo and Nita to drink, in the interests of making their doll act more convincing. The potion works, but the rest is accidentally drunk by every-one else, so that Alfredo and Ultrice believe they really are the Duke and Duchess, Minestra is an old woman, and the brigands have acquired monkish habits other than those they are wearing. Fortunately, the antidote is found, and, after brief panic when it appears to have been lost again, is used to restore everyone to normal.

PRINCIPAL NUMBERS

Act 1   '*Miserere, umbra frere*' (monks)
          'If you please' (Risotto and Minestra)
          'High Jerry ho!' (Arrostino and chorus)
          'Bedecked in fashion trim' (Alfredo)

The Mousmé (*The Maids of Japan*), *a musical play in three acts. Music by Lionel Monckton and Howard Talbot, book by Alexander M. Thompson and Robert Courtneidge, lyrics by Arthur Wimperis and Percy Greenbank. First produced: London, 1911. Set in Japan in 1904.* (Performing rights: Chappell & Co. Ltd.)

The Russo-Japanese War is imminent, and Japanese army officers have been ordered by their General to settle their debts before going into action. This is embarrassing for Captain Fujiwara, who cannot pay the three thousand yen he owes Captain Yamaki, his rival for O Hana San, a temple singer. Unknown to Fujiwara, Hana sells herself into the service of a tea-house keeper, Hashimoto, in order to raise the money. The debt is paid off and the soldiers depart for war.

When they return Yamaki promptly acquires O Hana San by buying the tea-house and her with it. Fujiwara desperately seeks to purchase her from his rival, who agrees to sell on condition that Fujiwara will offer no defence at the court martial that has been ordered on a charge trumped up by Yamaki to cover up his own cowardice in action. Although it will mean his professional ruin, Fujiwara accepts the bargain. He is saved, however, by a timely earthquake which demolishes the tea-house and, more importantly, gives time for another man, Suki, to return from the wars and reveal that Fujiwara is innocent and Yamaki guilty. Fujiwara at last learns how O Hana San had sacrificed herself for him, and they pledge their betrothal in the temple gardens. As a final payment for his villainy, Yamaki is deprived of the hand of the General's daughter, Miyoko, to whom he had been engaged all along, and she gives herself to another admirer, Makei.

PRINCIPAL NUMBERS

Act 1   'Honourable Jappy bride' (Miyoko)
         'I know nothing of life' (Hana)
         'Where, I wonder, can they be?' (Hana, Miyoko,
             Fujiwara and Makei)
         'Tho' I need no magic power' (Hana and Fujiwara)
Act 2   'Would you like to pick up?' (Tanaka)
         'Many little songs a maiden sings' (Hana and
             chorus)
         'I've faced some dangers terrible' (Suki and chorus)
         'Amorous youth in foreign parts' (Miyoko and
             Makei)
         'I haven't got a handsome face' (Hashimoto)
Act 3   'What romantic recollections' (Mitsu and Suki)
         'Happy little Jappy' (Miyoko and chorus)
         'Once there dwelt a little maiden' (Hana)

Mr Cinders, *a musical comedy in two acts. Music by Vivian Ellis and Richard Myers, book and lyrics by Clifford Grey and Greatrex Newman. First produced: London, 1929. Set in England in contemporary period.* (Performing rights: Macdonald & Young.)

This is a reworking of the traditional Cinderella story. Jim is an orphan under the care of his uncle and aunt, Sir George and Lady Lancaster, whose sons, Lumley and Guy, resent him. When Jim saves a local millionaire, Henry Kemp, from a watery death, Guy assumes the credit for the deed, seeking to impress Kemp's daughter Jill. Jill, however, takes a fancy to Jim, and when she learns that he has not been asked to the coming-of-age party her father is giving for her, she procures him an invitation and the fancy dress of an explorer.

Jim is introduced to the assembly as a real explorer, to his and everyone else's confusion. A crooked butler steals Jill's pearl necklace. Jim and Jill leap on to a motorbike and chase the man, cornering him at a remote railway station and retrieving the pearls. When the matter of a reward arises the police need to establish the veracity of the claimant by means of a bowler hat, found at the scene of the arrest. Guy and Lumley try it on, but it will fit neither. Like Cinderella's slipper, it fits Jim perfectly, and he gets both the reward and the heiress.

PRINCIPAL NUMBERS

Act 1 'Blue blood' (Guy, Lumley and girls)
'True to two' (Lumley and girls)
'I want the world to know' (Phyllis, Guy and chorus)

'One man girl' (Jim and Jill)
'On with the dance' (Minerva and chorus)
'Spread a little happiness' (Jill)
'Belles of the ball' (Lumley, Guy and Jim)
Act 2 'Jill' (Chorus)
'On the Amazon' (Jill and chorus)
'Every little moment' (Lumley and Minerva)
'I've got you – you've got me' (Jim and Jill)
'Honeymoon for four' (Lumley, Guy, Minerva and Phyllis)

My Fair Lady, *a musical play in two acts. Music by Frederick Loewe, book and lyrics by Alan Jay Lerner, based on Bernard Shaw's play* Pygmalion. *First produced: New York, 1956; London, 1958. Set in London and at Ascot in 1912.* (Performing rights: Evans Plays.)

A professor of phonetics, Henry Higgins, and his friend Colonel Pickering, strolling in Covent Garden market, encounter a thickly-accented Cockney flower-girl, Eliza Doolittle, and Pickering bets Higgins he cannot groom her in speech and manners to pass for a lady. Higgins takes her into his home and goes to work, undeterred by the importunings of her father, Alfred P. Doolittle, a coalman.

Eliza proves a difficult pupil, but at length the breakthrough is achieved with that tricky phrase 'The rain in Spain falls mainly on the plain', to which Eliza, Higgins and Pickering dance a triumphant tango. Afterwards Eliza muses on how she 'could have danced all night'. Higgins triumphantly produces her at Ascot, where, in her beautiful outfit and with her impeccable manners, she is admired by everyone, most of all by Freddy Eynsford-Hill, who thereafter pursues her ardently.

Her severest test is yet to come, at an Embassy ball. Once more Eliza carries it off superbly, but back at Higgins's afterwards rounds angrily on him and Pickering for turning her into something she is not. She storms out of the house to Covent Garden, where she meets her father, on his way to church to get married. Neither he nor her old friends recognize her: her disenchantment is complete.

Higgins, for all his confirmed bachelorhood, is missing her more than he cares to acknowledge. He meets her again, visiting his mother's house, and hears that Freddy Eynsford-Hill has asked her to marry him. He loses patience with her and they quarrel. But later that evening, lonely in his own home, Higgins sees Eliza come in quietly, and one knows that she is back to stay.

PRINCIPAL NUMBERS

Act 1   'Why can't the English?' (Higgins)
'Wouldn't it be loverly?' (Eliza and men)
'With a little bit of luck' (Doolittle, Jamie and Harry)
'I'm an ordinary man' (Higgins)
'Just you wait!' (Eliza)
'The rain in Spain' (Higgins, Eliza and Pickering)
'I could have danced all night' (Eliza, Mrs Pearce and maids)
'Ascot Gavotte' (chorus)
'On the street where you live' (Freddy)
The Embassy Waltz

Act 2 'You did it' (Higgins, Pickering and servants)
        'Show me' (Eliza and Freddy)
        'Get me to the church on time' (Doolittle and chorus)
        'Why can't a woman?' (Higgins)
        'Without you' (Eliza)
        'I've grown accustomed to her face' (Higgins)

My Lady Molly, *a comedy opera in two acts. Music by Sydney Jones, book and lyrics by G. H. Jessop, with additional lyrics by Percy Greenbank and Charles H. Taylor. First produced: London, 1903. Set in England in the 18th century.* (Performing rights: National Operatic and Dramatic Association.)

The course of true love, on the musical stage at least, seldom runs smoothly. The irascible squire, Sir Miles Coverdale, has a daughter, Alice, who has displeased him by falling in love with Lionel Bland, whereas Sir Miles intends her for Sir Harry Romney, son of an old friend of his, Judge Romney.

When Harry and his Irish servant, Mickey O'Dowd, arrive at the Coverdale Arms, Harry is smarting somewhat over his rejection by Lady Molly Martingale, a proud girl who nevertheless loves him to distraction. With her maid, Hester, she has plans for thwarting Sir Miles's match-making where Harry is concerned. Aided by Mickey, Molly dons a suit of Harry's (fortunately shrunk in the wash), attires Hester similarly and presents Harry's letter of credentials to Sir Miles, who has never seen Harry in person. The result is that when Lionel and Harry become

94

involved in a duel and Harry tries to present himself to Sir Miles, he is regarded as an impostor and arrested.

Meanwhile, Molly's male impersonation has proved so successful that she has Alice falling in love with her. Molly finds herself challenged to a duel by Harry and Judge Romney, a prospect that daunts her, despite the tuition Mickey gives her. Alice's unloved French governess, Mirabeau, has designs upon Sir Miles to which he succumbs. When all is at a height of confusion Judge Romney turns up and everything becomes sorted out, with Alice and Lionel pairing off, Molly getting her Harry at last, Mickey winning Hester, and Mirabeau, Sir Miles.

PRINCIPAL NUMBERS

Act 1   'A man may know no voice of friend' (Landlord)
'There's a little maid' (Lionel)
'The land of make-believe' (Alice and Lionel)
'Ballinasloe' (Mickey)
'Oh, I'll greet him soft and low' (Molly and Hester)
'Wear 'em wid an air' (Molly, Hester and Mickey)
'Hurrah for the field' (Sir Miles and chorus)
'The merry medieval maid' (Alice)
'To you, Sir Miles' (Harry)

Act 2   'I mean to be a good girl now' (Alice and chorus)
'Once too often' (Molly)
'Kiss, lad, and never tell' (Molly, Alice and Sir Miles)
'At my lady's feet' (Harry)
'Don't whistle so loud' (Mickey)
' 'Opeless ze state of me' (Mirabeau)

95

Naughty Marietta, *a musical play in two acts. Music by Victor Herbert, book and lyrics by Rida Johnson Young. First produced: New York, 1910. New version by Phil Park and Ronald Harmer, 1959. Set in New Orleans in the late 18th century.*

Marietta d'Altena, a Neapolitan who had run away from her native city to escape having to marry a man she did not want, has since come to New Orleans with a group of French girls, sent out to provide wives for Louisiana planters. Marriage has not yet caught up with her, however, when the tramp, tramp, tramp of marching feet resound through the town and soldiers enter the principal square. They are led by Captain Richard Warrington, popularly known as Captain Dick, who is on the track of a notorious pirate, 'Bras-Pique'.

Captain Dick quickly makes friends with Marietta, though he does not feel romantically towards her. One who does is the Lieutenant-Governor's son, Étienne Grandet, who is in turn loved by his quadroon slave, Adah. Étienne decides to disencumber himself of the adoring Adah, so he puts her up for auction. Captain Dick bids highest for her, in order to set the girl free from slavery, a gesture which is misinterpreted by Marietta, who believes he wants the girl for his own purposes. Jealously, she determines to accept Étienne's proposal of marriage.

Captain Dick realizes by now that he loves Marietta, but it seems it is too late to do anything about it. The grateful Adah clears the way for him by revealing that Étienne is the pirate Bras-Pique. The Lieutenant-Governor refuses to order his own son's arrest, but Étienne is just as effectively removed by having to fly from New Orleans, leaving Captain Dick and Marietta to express their devotion in the usual manner.

The Nautch Girl, *a comic opera in two acts. Music by Edward Solomon, book by George Dance, lyrics by George Dance and Frank Desprez. First produced: London, 1891. Set in an imaginary Indian province in contemporary period.* (Performing rights: Chappell & Co. Ltd.)

Indru, son of the Rajah Punka of Chutneypore, has fallen in love with a Nautch (dancing) girl, Beebee. Since the difference of their social levels forbids their marriage, Indru deliberately sacrifices caste by eating some potted cow in a public place. At that very moment, Beebee receives news that a long-standing lawsuit by her father to regain the high caste which he had lost accidentally years before has been settled in his favour. Consequently, it is now Beebee who is too high to marry Indru. Baboo Currie, the proprietor of the troupe with which she dances, offers to take them both to England where his girls are about to appear; but although Beebee escapes in this way, the Rajah's cousin, Pyjama, the despotic Grand Vizier, intercepts Indru and has him sentenced to six months' imprisonment, to be followed by death.

On the eve of Indru's execution he is rescued from his cell by Chinna Loofa, a poor girl relation of the Rajah. Grateful, but unresponsive to Chinna Loofa's hope that he will marry her, Indru makes himself scarce as people assemble to see the sacred idol, Bumba, carried on. The idol has come to life to upbraid the Rajah for having a son who could stoop so low as to want to marry a Nautch girl. He orders the execution of the Rajah and Indru and appoints Pyjama the new ruler. But it is Pyjama who is ultimately thrown to the crocodiles, for Beebee, returning from England in the nick of time, produces a splendid diamond, the idol's missing left eye, which Pyjama had stolen. The delighted Bumba restores the eye to its socket, permits Indru and Beebee to marry, and tells Chinna Loofa that if she will consent to being turned into wood he will marry her himself. She has no difficulty in agreeing.

PRINCIPAL NUMBERS

Act 1   'This is the place: Bow not good people' (Indru and chorus)

'The sun was setting' (Indru and chorus)

'Roses are fair' (Indru and Currie)

'One, two, three' (Beebee)

'And this is the royal diadem' (Punka and chorus)

'Now when a young man says . . .' (Punka, Beebee, Chinna and Pyjama)

'I can't help it' (Chinna)

Act 2 'The secret of my past success' (Pyjama and chorus)
'A little caged bird' (Indru and Chinna)
'It was all my eye' (Bumba)
'Put upon the shelf' (Bumba and chorus)
'Vive la liberté' (Chinna and Bumba)
'Crocodile' (Bumba, Punka, Chinna)
'Near thee once more' (Beebee)
'When all the world was bright' (Indru)

The New Moon, *a romantic musical in two acts. Music by Sigmund Romberg, book and lyrics by Oscar Hammerstein II, Frank Mandel and Laurence Schwab. First produced: New York, 1928; London, 1929. Set in New Orleans and on the Caribbean Sea in 1792–3.* (Performing rights: Chappell & Co. Ltd.)

At the end of the 18th century there was published the account by Robert Mission, a French aristocrat, of his adventurous experiences in New Orleans and the Caribbean, from which work *The New Moon* is freely derived.

The musical opens in the New Orleans home of a rich shipowner, Beaunoir, in whose service Robert Mission is keeping out of the authorities' notice after fleeing from France. A sinister Vicomte Ribaud is on his track, with orders to take him back for trial for revolutionary activities. Captain Duval, the master of the ship *The New Moon*, which has brought Ribaud from France, is in love with Beaunoir's daughter Marianne, but she finds him tedious and much less attractive than her father's curiously well-bred bond-servant, Robert.

Robert is duly detected and taken aboard *The New Moon*,

99

which sails for France with Marianne also on board. However, in the Caribbean the ship is attacked by pirates. When Captain Duval hoists the white flag of surrender, Robert intervenes, beats off the pirates and takes command.

The party sets up a little colony of their own on the Isle of Pines. Ribaud tries to create a mutiny, in order to depose Robert as leader and surrender to a French ship lying nearby. But the ship's captain reveals that Louis XVI is dead and France is now a republic, so that Ribaud is confounded and Robert and Marianne and all the others are free to do as they choose.

PRINCIPAL NUMBERS

Act 1   'Marianne' (Robert)
        'The girl on the prow' (Marianne, Besac and chorus)
        'Gorgeous Alexander' (Julie and Alexander, with girls)
        'I'm seeking the hand of a maiden' (Marianne, Duval and Robert)
        'Softly, as in a morning sunrise' (Philippe and chorus)
        'Stout-hearted men' (Robert and Philippe)
        'One kiss' (Marianne and girls)
        'Wanting you' (Marianne and Robert)
Act 2   'Funny little sailormen' (Clotilde, Besac and chorus)
        'Lover come back to me' (Marianne)
        'Love is quite a simple thing' (Julie, Alexander, Besac and Clotilde)
        'Try her out at dances' (Julie and Alexander)
        'Never for you' (Marianne)

No, No, Nanette, *a musical comedy in three acts. Music by Vincent Youmans, book by Otto Harbach and Frank Mandel, based on the play,* His Lady Friends, *by Emile Nyitray and Frank Mandel, with lyrics by Irving Caesar and Otto Harbach. First produced: London, 1925; New York, 1925. Set in America in contemporary period.* (Performing rights: Samuel French Ltd.)

Being a publisher of Bibles does not inhibit Billy Early from appreciating the company of ladies, preferably young and attractive ones. His daughter Nanette takes after him in temperament, loving fun and parties and staying out until all hours, despite the disapproval of her somewhat serious-minded fiancé, Tom, who, however, loves and understands her enough to believe that she is passing through an essential phase, from which she will eventually emerge in a mood to marry him and settle down. A development to give him more than usual concern is a flirtation she seems to be having with her father's lawyer, Jimmy Smith.

Another concerned person is Lucille Early, Billy's wife and Nanette's mother. She know all about her husband's propensities, but objects strongly when, during a family holiday to Atlantic City, he takes on three lively girls, Betty, Flora and Winnie, simultaneously. Jimmy Smith persuades them to accept cash in lieu of his employer's attentions, and they depart happily, leaving Billy to face his wife's demand that he spend his money on her in future. Meanwhile, Nanette manages to reassure Tom that there is nothing between Jimmy and her, and that the prospect of Tom's dream of 'Tea for two' becoming reality was never stronger. (N.B. The revised version presented in the U.S.A. and U.K. in the 1970s differs considerably.)

Act 1 'The call of the sea' (Billy)

'Too many rings around Rosie' (Lucille and chorus)

'I've confessed to the breeze' (Nanette and Tom)

'I want to be happy' (Nanette, Jimmy and chorus)

'No, No, Nanette' (Nanette and chorus)

Act 2 'Fight over me' (Betty, Winnie and Jimmy)

'Tea for two' (Nanette and Tom)

'You can dance with any girl' (Lucille and Billy)

Act 3 'Take a little one-step' (Nanette and Billy)

Oklahoma!, *a musical play in two acts. Music by Richard Rodgers, book and lyrics by Oscar Hammerstein II, based on the play,* Green Grow the Lilacs, *by Lynn Riggs. First produced: New York, 1943; London, 1947. Set in rural territory of Oklahoma in the early 20th century.* (Performing rights: Williamson Music Limited.)

Singing 'Oh, what a beautiful mornin'' as he approaches, an impecunious farm boy, Curly, comes to Aunt Eller's in the hope that he can persuade her niece, Laurey, to come to a local dance with him that evening. Laurey is fonder of Curly than she would admit, but her pride will not let her give way to his blandishments. She spites him deliberately by choosing to go to the dance with another man, Jud Fry, an uncouth hired-hand. Curly makes a show of independence by letting it be known that he will take another girl to the dance instead.

This dance is causing ructions in the neighbourhood. Will Parker, triumphantly back from Kansas City with the fifty dollars Judge Andrew Carnes has challenged him to earn before he will let him have his daughter, Ado Annie, finds that a Persian pedlar, Hakim, has been after his girl in his absence, and that he is her chosen partner for the evening. Worse still, her father is pressing the pair to marry.

But three weeks later Curly and Laurey marry. Jud forces his way into their celebrations and draws a knife on Curly, but in the struggle which ensues it is Jud who accidentally gets the knife in him and dies. At a summary trial conducted by Judge Carnes, Curly is acquitted. He and Laurey are free to start their life together, and it is plain that Will Parker will marry his Ado Annie after all.

PRINCIPAL NUMBERS

Act 1 'Oh, what a beautiful mornin'' (Curly)
      'The Surrey with the fringe on top' (Curly, Laurey and Aunt Eller)
      'Kansas City' (Will, Aunt Eller and boys)
      'I cain't say no' (Ado Annie)
      'Many a new day' (Laurey and girls)
      'It's a scandal! It's a outrage' (Ali Hakim and boys and girls)
      'People will say we're in love' (Curly and Laurey)
      'Poor Jud is daid' (Curly and Jud)
      'Lonely room' (Jud)
      'Out of my dreams' (Laurey and girls)
      Laurey makes up her mind (Ballet)
Act 2 'The farmer and the cowman' (Chorus)
      'All er nothin'' (Ado Annie)
      'Oklahoma!' (Curly, Laurey, Aunt Eller, Ike, Fred and ensemble)

Old Chelsea, *a musical romance in three acts. Music by Richard Tauber, book by Walter Ellis, lyrics by Fred S. Tysh and Walter Ellis, with additional numbers by Bernard Grun. First produced: London, 1943. Set in Chelsea at the end of the 18th century.* (Performing rights: Samuel French Ltd.)

Lord Ranelagh has been persuaded by a charming little Chelsea milliner, Mary Fenton, to listen to a new opera composed by the penniless man she adores, Jacob Bray. Unluckily, Ranelagh prematurely overhears some very slipshod rehearsal work, and does not conceal his derision. Not knowing the interloper's identity, Jacob berates him and Ranelagh retires in a huff.

The rehearsal continues, however, and improves in quality. It is overheard this time by another stranger, Nancy Gibbs, a famous operatic singer. Much impressed, she joins in the performance and then tells Jacob she will appear in his work. The only obstacle to this is that Lord Ranelagh happens to be both her sponsor and her lover: it is not easy to persuade him to hear the work again, but when he does he recognizes its quality and agrees to support it.

Preparations for its performance throw Jacob and Nancy much together, to the exclusion of Mary. So much so, that when Lord Ranelagh returns from an absence he hears gossip about the association between the two. He accuses Nancy, and gives her an ultimatum: either she gives up her part in the opera, or he will leave her. She does not have to make the choice, however, for Ranelagh suffers an accident and Nancy hurries away to care for him, leaving Jacob without his principal singer. Jacob despairingly goes home, convinced that Fate has deliberately cheated him. Unbeknown to him, his conductor, Peter Crawley, substitutes Mary for Nancy and the performance goes on, with the result that Mary is acclaimed a great discovery, the work is declared a masterpiece, and Mary and Jacob are reunited in love.

PRINCIPAL NUMBERS

Act 1 'Music in my heart' (Jacob)
     'A holiday for Chelsea' (Peter, Christine and chorus)
     'My heart and I' (Mary, Jacob and ensemble)
Act 2 'Just a little gossip' (Lady Walgrave, Countess of Stafford, Sir Percy and Sir Roger)
     'If you are in love' (Jacob and Nancy)
     'There are angels outside Heaven' (Nancy, Mary and Jacob)
     'Your love could mean everything to me' (Jacob)
     'Why did I have to awake from my dream?' (Mary)
Act 3 'Three cheers for tonight' (Ensemble)
     'Do you know?' (Nancy and Ranelagh)

Our Miss Gibbs, *a musical play in two acts. Music by Ivan Caryll and Lionel Monckton, book by 'Cryptos' and James T. Tanner, lyrics by Adrian Ross and Percy Greenbank. First produced: London, 1909, and set in London in that year.* (Performing rights: Emile Littler Musical Plays.)

Mary Gibbs is the pretty Yorkshire manageress of the flower department of a London store. Many wealthy young men-about-town admire her, especially Lord Eynsford, son of the Earl of St Ives, who prefers to let her believe he is a mere bank clerk. His fiancée, Lady Betty Thanet, whom he has no wish to marry, is in love with the Hon. Hughie Pierrepoint, who fancies himself as a gentleman burglar and is pursuing an apprenticeship under a professional crook, Slithers.

Hughie has just pulled off his greatest coup, the theft of the Ascot Gold Cup from Lord St Ives's house, when he meets Mary Gibbs's ingenuous cousin Timothy, up from Yorkshire, who carries a suitcase identical to the one in which Hughie has the cup. Each gets the other's case, and Slithers, seeing Timothy examining with astonishment the unexpected contents of his, quickly finds a way of tricking him out of possession of the cup.

Betty Thanet frees Lord Eynsford from his engagement to her, but Mary has discovered that he is not the simple clerk he had pretended to be and rejects him for deceiving her. She gives up her job and embarks upon a life in Society. At the Franco-British Exhibition in London she and Timothy meet Lord St Ives, who tells them he is determined to hound down the thief of the Ascot Gold Cup. A police description of the wanted man is too like Timothy for his comfort, so he disguises himself as one of the runners in the Windsor-to-London Marathon race. The crowd at the finish mistake him for the winner, then duck him in a lake when they find he is not. But he is compensated for his troubles when Slithers, who has been given five hundred pounds by Hughie for the return of the Gold Cup, shares the money with Timothy. Lord St Ives gets his cup back, and Mary, learning that Lord Eynsford's deceit had been practised out of genuine devotion for her, takes him back, too.

Act 1   'My Yorkshire lassie' (Eynsford)
'Hats' (Jeanne and girls)
'Romance' (Betty)
'Correct' (Chorus of Dudes)
'Mary – people call me pretty Mary' (Mary and Dudes)
'Hughie' (Hughie and chorus)
'Country cousins' (Mary and Timothy)
'Not that sort of person' (Mary and Hughie)
Act 2   'Yip-iaddy-i-ay' (Hughie)
'In Yorkshire' (Mary)
'An English gentleman' (Hughie, Slithers, Eynsford, Timothy and others)
'Our farm' (Mary and Timothy)
'Moonstruck' ('I'm such a silly when the moon comes out') (Mary and girls)
'You come and stay with me' (Hughie and Timothy)

The Pajama Game, *a musical in two acts. Music and lyrics by Richard Adler and Jerry Ross, book by George Abbott and Richard Bissell, based on Richard Bissell's novel, 7½ Cents. First produced: New York, 1954; London, 1955. Set in Cedar Rapids, Ohio, in contemporary period.* (Performing rights: Frank Music Co. Limited.)

Labour relations are not good at the pajama-making factory managed by Hasler and superintended by Sid Sorokin. Sid is new to the job, and an early visitor to his office is Babe Williams, head of the grievance committee of union members. Her mission is to plead her fellow-workers' case for another $7\frac{1}{2}$ cents an hour, but Sid's mind dwells more on the attractive girl herself and he tries to make a date with her. He fails, but she is not unaware of his personal qualities and at a staff picnic does not resist when his kiss takes her by surprise.

Attempts by Sid to follow up his advantage are unsuccessful, however. Babe makes it plain that her union's fight is what comes first with her, and that she can submerge her feelings for Sid beneath it. A showdown between them is precipitated when Sid threatens the sack for workers who are going slow in protest and Babe brings the machinery to a halt with a well-placed kick.

Desperate to make it up with Babe and certain that there is some secret behind the management's refusal to budge on the terms, Sid takes Hasler's book-keeper, Gladys, to a night-spot, Hernando's Hideaway, and plies her with liquor and blandishments until she willingly gives him the key to the company's records. There, Sid finds evidence that Hasler himself has been pocketing the $7\frac{1}{2}$ cents each worker might have had. The workers are triumphant at last, and Babe is only too pleased to come to terms with Sid.

PRINCIPAL NUMBERS

Act 1   'I'm not at all in love' (Babe, Poopsie and girls)
'I'll never be jealous again' (Mabel and Hines)
'Hey there!' (Sid)
'Her is' (Chorus)
'Once-a-year day' (Sid, Babe, Poopsie and chorus)
'There once was a man' ('I love you more') (Sid and Babe)

A Princess of Kensington, *a comic opera in two acts. Music by Edward German, book and lyrics by Basil Hood. First produced: London, 1903. Set in Kensington Gardens and in the fishing village of 'Winklemouth' in contemporary period.* (Performing rights: Chappell & Co. Ltd.)

It is Midsummer Day and the fairies are gathered in Kensington Gardens, preparing to enjoy their once-yearly privilege of assuming mortal shape. One of them, Azuriel, is apprehensive. His love is Kenna, the Princess of Kensington, who had once been mortal but had changed into a fairy after the death of her mortal lover, Prince Albion. Azuriel has learnt that Albion's death had been changed by fairy processes into 1,000 years' sleep, which is now almost over, and he fears that when Albion awakes he will reclaim Kenna from him.

As a scheme to persuade Azuriel that Albion has already reawakened and married another mortal, Puck, the Imp of Mischief, finds four sailors with H.M.S. *Albion* inscribed on their hats, selects one of them, William Jelf, whom he hopes Azuriel will take to be Prince Albion, and arranges for the man to meet a girl named Joy Jellicoe, whose banker father has recently given his consent to her engagement with his clerk, Brook Green. Puck assumes her father's form and tells her he desires her to marry Jelf instead.

Puck has overlooked the fact that Jelf is engaged to Nell Reddish, daughter of the landlord of the Jolly Tar inn at Winklemouth, who now turns up to claim him. Azuriel hastily assumes the form of a Judge and decrees that Jelf must marry both girls, which ruling causes Joy to run away.

Joy chances to finish up in Winklemouth, where she gets a job as a maid at Nell's father's inn. Brook follows, disguised as a fisherman; and Puck, too, is there, as a Registrar, waiting to perform instant marriages. But Jelf meets Azuriel and assures him that he is not Prince Albion and has no intention of marrying Kenna. Kenna and Azuriel thankfully revert to fairy form, and, after further complications, Joy and Brook are firmly reunited.

PRINCIPAL NUMBERS

Act 1 'From where the Scotch mountains' (Oberon and Titania)

'If we pass beyond the portals' (Puck and chorus)

'Seven o'clock in the morning' (Joy and Brook)

'We're four jolly sailormen' (Jelf and sailors)

'Oh! What is a woman's duty?' (Nell)

'Now here's to the 'prentices' (Brook and chorus)

'A sailorman's the sort of man' (Jelf)

Act 2 'A mountain stood like a grim outpost' (Kenna)

'My heart a ship at anchor lies' (Brook)

'He was a simple sailorman' (Joy)

The Quaker Girl, *a musical play in three acts. Music by Lionel Monckton, book by James T. Tanner, lyrics by Adrian Ross and Percy Greenbank. First produced: London, 1910. Revised version by Emile Littler, 1944. Set in an English village and Paris in the mid-19th century.* (Performing rights: Emile Littler Musical Plays.)

A non-Quaker wedding is about to take place in a Quaker-dominated village in England. The Princess Mathilde, exiled from France for Bonapartist sympathies, has come here to marry an Englishman, Captain Charteris. They are accompanied by the Princess's close friend, Madame Blum, a fashionable Paris *couturière*, and Charteris's Best Man, Tony Chute, an American from his country's Embassy in Paris. The latter is immediately attracted by the beauty of Prudence Pym, the niece of the two Quaker elders, and she proves susceptible both to his charms and to the allurements of a gayer way of life. When Madame Blum, recognizing a new fashion for Paris in the simple Quaker dress, invites Prudence to return with her as model, she agrees readily.

The dress takes Paris by storm. Unhappily for Tony, Prudence herself attracts many admirers, prominent among whom is the lady-killing Prince Carlo. His debonair manner and expensive habits fascinate her, and she willingly accepts his invitation to a ball he is giving. Tony begs her not to go, but the Prince threatens that if she does not attend he will disclose to the police that Princess Mathilde, who has secretly returned to France, is posing as a model at Madame Blum's. To save the Princess, Prudence promises to be at the ball.

Princess Mathilde also attends the ball, with the object

of speaking to Minister Duhamel, the only person with power to rescind her banishment. He, too, is in pursuit of Prudence, and has promised to grant her any favour. An actress named Diane, who is jealous of Tony Chute's attachment to Prudence, slips some of her love-letters from Tony into the pocket of Prudence's dress, hoping that they will make Prudence break from Tony; but Duhamel has been another of Diane's admirers, and it is his letters to her that the actress has mistakenly planted on Prudence. When the latter finds them she hands them back unconditionally to Duhamel, although he has just broken his promise by refusing her request that Princess Mathilde be pardoned. Realizing that Prudence could have blackmailed him, but had made no attempt to do so, Duhamel is touched and agrees to let the Princess stay. When he hears the facts, Tony, who had been angered by Prudence's seeming preference for Prince Carlo, is gladly reconciled with her.

PRINCIPAL NUMBERS

Act 1 'Quakers meeting' (Chorus)
'O time, time!' (Mathilde)
'A runaway match' (Mathilde, Phoebe, Charteris, Tony)
'A Quaker girl' (Prudence)
'The bad boy and the good girl' (Prudence and Tony)
'Tiptoe' (Chorus)
'Just as father used to do' (Jerry and chorus)
Act 2 'Or thereabouts' (Phoebe)
'Come to the ball' (Prince Carlo and chorus)
'A dancing lesson' (Prudence and Tony)
'Barbizon' (Ensemble)

Act 3 'Couleur de rose' (Prince Carlo and chorus)
'Mr Jeremiah, Esquire' (Phoebe and Jerry)
'Tony from America' (Prudence)

The Rebel Maid, *a romantic light opera in three acts. Music by Montague Phillips, book by Alexander M. Thompson, lyrics by Gerald Dodson. First produced: London, 1921. Set in Devonshire in 1688.* (Performing rights: Chappell & Co. Ltd.)

Popular resentment against King James II of England is rife, and the Prince of Orange has been invited by the rebel movement to invade the country and restore its people's liberties. Sir Stephen Crespigny, appointed by the King to investigate reports of secret landings of men and arms in Devonshire, is staying with his uncle, Lord Milverton, Lord Lieutenant of the county, at whose house he meets the young and beautiful Lady Mary Trefusis and falls in love with her. But Lord Milverton's son, the Hon. Derek Lanscombe, has known Mary since childhood, and when he lands from his sailing boat and re-encounters her at his father's garden-party they both know that old acquaintance has given way to love. Neither dares reveal to the other that they are working for the rebel cause: Mary is the local leader, 'Snow Bunting', the Rebel Maid; Derek is waiting to pilot the Prince of Orange's fleet safely into port to coincide with the uprising.

Sir Stephen has his suspicions of both and they fall together into a trap he sets at a local inn after intercepting a message about arrangements for the landing. Luckily, the fishermen thronging the inn all hold rebellious sympathies. They overpower Sir Stephen's soldiers, and Mary's maid Abigail shows Derek the way to safety through a secret tunnel.

Mary remains, though. Sir Stephen offers an ultimatum: either she consents to marry him or he will have Derek shot the moment he is seen. When Lord Milverton tries to intervene, Sir Stephen adds the further condition that if Mary will not marry him he will have her tried for high treason.

As Sir Stephen has anticipated, Derek comes to find Mary, and is seized. News is brought that Prince William has landed. Sir Stephen orders Derek's immediate execution; but before it can be carried out Prince William arrives in person and Derek is saved for Mary, and to sing his well-known song 'The Fishermen of England'.

PRINCIPAL NUMBERS

Act 1 'In 1688' (Dorothy and Percy)
   'Sunshine and laughter' (Mary and chorus)
   'Shepherdess and Beau Brocade' (Mary, Dorothy, Percy and Derek)
   'I know there'll be trouble for me' (Solomon)
   'Unavailing little lady' (Derek and chorus)
   'When we get back to Dorset' (Abigail and Solomon)
   'When a dream of love you cherish' (Mary)
Act 2 'The old-fashioned cloak' (Mary)
   'Are my lanterns shining?' (Mary and chorus)
   'Cautious' (Abigail, Solomon and Bunkle)
   'Now we stand on the summit of the hill' (Mary and Derek)
Act 3 'Sail my ships' (Mary)
   'The Fishermen of England' (Derek and chorus)

Rose Marie, *a musical play in two acts. Music by Herbert Stothart and Rudolf Friml, book and lyrics by Otto Harbach and Oscar Hammerstein II. First produced: New York, 1924; London, 1925. Set in the Rocky Mountains of Canada in contemporary period.* (Performing rights: Samuel French Ltd.)

When Jim Kenyon arrived in Canada to seek his fortune he lived up to his nickname 'Wild Jim', in ample measure. He has quietened down considerably since, though, and it is all attributable to his new-found love for Rose Marie la Flamme, a singer at a Saskatchewan saloon run by 'Lady Jane'. Her return of his affections has gained him a cunning enemy in a rich man, Ed Hawley, who wants Rose himself, and is determined to get her.

Hawley's chance seems to have come when a villainous half-breed, Black Eagle, is found murdered in his remote cabin. It is well known that there had been bitterness between him and Jim Kenyon over a mining claim, and Jim is believed to have been the last person to visit Black Eagle. Hawley makes sure that the attention of the Royal Canadian Mounted Police, under Sergeant Malone, is drawn to these details, and nothing Jim or his well-meaning but bungling friend, 'Hard-boiled Herman', can do can save him from arrest.

Rose Marie knows that Hawley could tell what really happened to Black Eagle, and offers herself to him if he will do it. But there is no need: the Mounties have uncovered the truth Hawley is hiding – that the man had been knifed by his own Indian wife, Wanda, who is in love with Hawley.

Act 1 'Hard-boiled Herman' (Herman and girls)
      'Rose Marie' (Jim and Malone)
      'The Mounties' (Malone and boys)
      'Lak Jeem' (Rose Marie and boys)
      'Indian love call' (Rose Marie and Jim)
      'Pretty things' (Rose Marie and chorus)
      'Why shouldn't we?' (Jane and Herman)
      'Totem Tom-Tom' (Wanda and chorus)
Act 2 'Only a kiss' (Jane, Herman and Malone)
      'The door of my dreams' (Rose Marie)
      'Dear place where once I thought' (Jim)

The Rose of Persia, *a comic opera in two acts. Music by Arthur Sullivan, book and lyrics by Basil Hood. First produced: London, 1899. Set in Persia in olden times.* (Performing rights: Bridget D'Oyly Carte Limited.)

A rich and eccentric merchant, Abu-el-Hassan, enjoys entertaining beggars, dancing-girls and idlers in his resplendent home, where a teller of romantic stories, Yussuf, entertains them with tales in instalments, along the lines of the *Arabian Nights*. The Sultan, curious to see some of these types for himself, sends the priest Abdullah to the house to collect a few.

What the Sultan does not know is that his Sultana, Rose-in-Bloom, is an habituée of the house, in the guise of a dancing-girl and accompanied by three of her favourite female slaves. One of the slaves, Heart's Desire, has fallen in love with Yussuf. It is she who, when Abdullah and the constabulary arrive, saves the Sultana from detection.

Abu-el-Hassan, apprehensive of troubles in store, doses himself with the drug 'bhang' and lapses into a state of unconcerned elation.

The Sultan himself arrives to find out what is going on, and proceeds to amuse himself by having Hassan transported to the palace, attired in royal robes, and placed on the throne, where he wakes up at length still influenced by the drug and believing himself to be Sultan. Abdullah has meanwhile discovered the Sultana's secret and reports to his master, who orders death sentences all round. The slave, Heart's Desire, saves the situation yet again by pursuading him that Yussuf's series of tales can hardly be allowed to end unhappily, and since death is an unhappy ending, the one thing inevitably implies the other; therefore the stories should be allowed to go on and Yussuf's audience retained intact. This syllogistic form of reasoning appeals to the Sultan, and all are pardoned.

PRINCIPAL NUMBERS

Act 1 'I'm Abu-el-Hassan' (Hassan)

'When Islam first arose' (Abdullah and girls)

'O life has put it into my hand' (Dancing Sunbeam)

'If you ask me to advise you' (Rose-in-Bloom, Scent-of-Lilies and Heart's Desire)

' 'Neath my lattice through the night' (Rose-in-Bloom)

'When my father sent me to Ispahan' (Hassan and chorus)

'Musical maidens are we' (Ensemble with dancers)

'We have come to invade' (Abdullah, Hassan and chorus)

'Attended by these palace warders' (Grand Vizier, Physician, Executioner and chorus)

Salad Days, *a musical comedy in two acts. Music by Julian Slade, book and lyrics by Dorothy Reynolds and Julian Slade. First produced: Bristol, 1954; London, 1954. Set in an English university city and in London in contemporary period.* (Performing rights: Samuel French Ltd.)

Timothy and Jane have just graduated from their university and make plans to meet again in London, where their respective parents live. They are apprehensive that they will be made to take different directions in life, which, indeed, proves to be Timothy's case, for he has plenty of uncles with influence, through one or another of whom he is expected to find a position. He meets Jane and they agree that their best plan for staying together would be the *fait accompli* of marriage. They carry this off, but there remains the problem of making their living.

They encounter in St James's Park a tramp with a street piano, which he proceeds to play so infectiously that they are compelled to dance. Timothy is allowed to try his hand at the piano, and soon everyone in the park is dancing.

The tramp has offered to pay Timothy and Jane £7 a week to look after his piano – referred to as 'Minnie' – for a month. A little dumb man named Troppo who takes over at night manages to convey a warning to them that the Minister of Pastimes and Pleasures, who by nature is the very opposite of what his title implies, is leading a search for this piano which is reported to be provoking so much enjoyment. The Minister's personal pleasure is ogling a nightclub singer, Asphyxia, every night. Timothy and Jane try to take a compromising photograph of him with which to defend 'Minnie', but fail, and the Minister tracks them down to the park. Troppo hides 'Minnie' just in time, but loses her. It takes the aid of a flying saucer to locate the piano, restore her to her owner, and gain, through her irresistible music, Timothy's and Jane's parents' approval of their marriage.

PRINCIPAL NUMBERS

Act 1	'We said we wouldn't look back' (Jane and Timothy)
	'I'll sit in the sun' (Jane)
	'Oh, look at me' (Jane and Timothy)
	'Hush-hush' (Uncle Clem, Fosdyke and Timothy)
Act 2	'Sand in my eyes' (Asphyxia)
	'We're looking for a piano' (Jane, Fiona, Timothy, Nigel, Constable Boot, Gus, Pressmen and chorus)
	'The time of my life' (Jane)
	'We don't understand our children' (Timothy's and Jane's mothers)

Sally, *a musical play in three acts. Music by Jerome Kern, with additional music by Victor Herbert, book and lyrics by Guy Bolton and Clifford Grey. First produced: New York, 1920; London, 1921. A new version, revised by Frank Eyton and Richard Hearne, was presented in London in 1942 with the title* Wild Rose. *Set in Long Island in contemporary period.* (Performing rights: Emile Littler Musical Plays.)

The thin story contains one generally irresistible ingredient – the rise of a good, pretty little girl from rags to riches. In this case she is Sally, the poor washer-up at a restaurant in Long Island, where she is befriended by one of the waiters, Constantine, a Balkan nobleman who had found a haven in America after a revolution had forced him to leave his own country. Determined to help her, he persuades her to assume the identity of a Russian ballerina and gets her into a fashionable party being given by a millionaire, Otis Hooper. Her dancing charms everyone, and leads to stardom with the *Ziegfeld Follies* and marriage with a rich and eligible young man, Blair Farquar.

PRINCIPAL NUMBERS

Act 1   'It's the night walk that we love' (Jimmie and
            chorus)
         'On with the dance' (Otis)
         'You can't keep a good girl down' (Sally)
         'Look for the silver lining' (Sally and Blair)
         'A heartful of joy and gladness' (Sally)
         'Sally' (Blair and men)

Act 2   'Wild rose' (Sally and men)
       'The Schnitza-Komisski' (Constantine)
       'Whip-poor-will' (Sally and Blair)
       'The Lorelei' (Rosie, Jimmie and Otis)
       'The church round the corner' (Rosie and Otis)
Act 3   The Butterfly Ballet

San Toy, *a musical comedy in two acts. Music by Sidney Jones, book by Edward Morton, lyrics by Harry Greenbank and Adrian Ross. First produced: London, 1899. Set in China in contemporary period.* (Performing rights: Emile Littler Musical Plays.)

San Toy is the pretty daughter of a wealthy Mandarin, Yen How, of the city of Pynka Pong. Although she is anything but amazonian, she is one of those who receive a command from the Emperor to enlist in his female bodyguard, 'The Emperor's Own', a destiny which her father tries to save her from by dressing her as a boy and pretending she is his son. The disguise does not deceive Bobbie Preston, the son of the British Consul, who is engaged to give San Toy English lessons, and they are soon in love with one another. Another loving couple are Bobbie's sister Poppy and Lieutenant Harry Tucker.

Yen How has arranged that San Toy shall marry a student, Fo Hop, so that, as a wife, she will not be required to respond to the Emperor's summons. Fo Hop is so little to San Toy's taste that she prefers to go to Pekin and obey the Emperor. Bobbie, who has to go there on official business, accompanies her, to the fury of Fo Hop, who reveals how Yen How had been deceiving his Emperor.

The Emperor duly summons Yen How to Pekin to explain himself. The latter hastily dispatches a courier, Li, to say that he is sending his son, San Toy, to His Majesty; but San Toy has already reached Pekin and has presented herself to the Emperor as the girl she really is. Li is arrested when he arrives with the untruthful note, but escapes through the contrivance of Poppy Preston's maid Dudley, who dresses Li as one of 'The Emperor's Own'.

Charmed by San Toy, the Emperor briefly contemplates making her one of his wives. On reflection, he finds her English tastes and habits uncongenial. Bobbie Preston, who does not, quickly claims her for his own.

PRINCIPAL NUMBERS

Act 1 'The lady's maid' (Dudley)
'A posy from over the sea' (Poppy)
'Six little wives' (Yen How and Wives)
'The petals of the plum tree' (San Toy)
'A.B.C.' (San Toy and Bobbie)
'Love has come from Lotus Land' (Bobbie)
'Pynka Pong' (Quartette)
'Samee gamee' (Dudley and Li)
'Me gettee out very quick' (Li)
Act 2 'Rhoda and her pagoda' (Dudley)
'The little China maid' (San Toy and Bobbie)
'Sons of the Motherland' (Bobbie)
'We have come to see' (Six Wives)
'Back to London' (Quartette and chorus)
'I mean to introduce it into China' (Yen How)

The Shop Girl, *a musical farce in two acts. Music by Ivan Caryll, with additional numbers by Adrian Ross and Lionel Monckton; book and lyrics by H. J. W. Dam. First produced: London, 1894. A revised version with additional music by Herman Darewski was presented in London in 1920. Set in London in contemporary period.* (Performing rights: Emile Littler Musical Plays.)

When John Brown left England for Colorado he travelled steerage. When he returns he occupies a luxury suite, for in the years between he has risen from miner to millionaire. Wealth has not deprived him of his integrity, though, and he has come back primarily to look for the daughter of a fellow miner, to whom a fortune of four million pounds is due.

Brown advertises for her to come forward, mentioning a birth-mark on her shoulder. One who sees the advertisement is Mr Hooley, proprietor of the Royal Stores in London, who happens to know that one of his apprentices, Ada Smith, has such a birth-mark and is of obscure parentage. Although she is engaged to Mr Miggles, his shopwalker, Hooley determines to run no risk of missing out on a wife with four million pounds attached to her, and proposes to Ada, who accepts him. He comes unstuck, though. There is another shop girl, Bessie Brent, who is hoping to marry a young and impecunious medical student, Charles Appleby, whose high-placed family disapprove of the match. It is Bessie who proves to be the heiress, and when they learn the size of her inheritance Charles's family's objections dissolve remarkably swiftly.

Act 1 'By special appointments' (Hooley, Bessie and chorus)
'Superfluous relations' (Charles)
'I stand at my counter' (Bessie)
'Over the hills' (Beatrice)
'Foundlings are we' (Ensemble)
'The vegetarian' (Miggles)

Act 2 'Love on the Japanese plan' (Miggles and Miss Robinson)
'Brown of Colorado' (Brown)
'Too clever by half' (Sir George, Count de Vaurien, Appleby, Singleton and Colonel)
'Beautiful, bountiful Bertie' (Bertie)

Show Boat, *a musical play in two acts, based on Edna Ferber's novel of the same title. Music by Jerome Kern, book and lyrics by Oscar Hammerstein II. First produced: New York, 1927; London, 1928. Set at Natchez, Mississippi, and Chicago at the end of the 19th century.* (Performing rights: Chappell & Co. Ltd.)

Unlike most of the young ladies aboard the show boat *Cotton Blossom*, which cruises the Mississippi dispensing entertainment to the riverside communities, Magnolia is neither actress nor singer, but the daughter of the boat's master, Captain Andy. She longs to be an entertainer, though, and is encouraged in this aim by the handsome but unreliable Gaylord Ravenal, a gambler with whom she falls in love at first sight. She seeks an opinion of Gaylord from Joe, a member of the crew, but he evades having to answer by singing philosophically of 'Ol' Man River'.

Julie, the show boat's star performer, is more forthright, however, and tries to warn Magnolia.

Julie and her husband are unable at the last moment to take part in the show. (In the original version this was because Julie was a Negress and her husband a white man, a combination not permitted at Natchez, but *Show Boat* today is more often performed by all-white casts.) Magnolia and Gaylord fill their places, their performance culminating in mutual declarations of love and a decision to marry.

Some years later Captain Andy visits his daughter in Chicago, to learn that Gaylord's gambling is ruining life for Magnolia and her daughter Kim. When Gaylord deserts them Magnolia looks for work as a singer, finding it through the unselfishness of Julie, who learns of her plight and gives up her own singing engagement, enabling Magnolia to make a big success in her place. But Captain Andy returns to take Magnolia and Kim back to the show boat, where they find a repentant Gaylord awaiting them, and Ol' Man River still 'rollin' along'.

PRINCIPAL NUMBERS

Act 1 'Make believe' (Gaylord and Magnolia)
    'Ol' Man River' (Joe and men)
    'Can't help lovin' that man' (Julie, Queenie, Magnolia, Joe and others)
    'Life on the wicked stage' (Ellie and girls)
    'Till good luck comes my way' (Gaylord and men)
    'You are love' (Gaylord and Magnolia)
Act 2 'Why do I love you?' (Magnolia, Gaylord, Captain Andy, Parthy and chorus)
    'He's just my Bill' (Julie)
    'After the ball' (Magnolia)
    'Dance away the night' (Kim and chorus)

The Sound of Music, *a musical in two acts. Music by Richard Rodgers, lyrics by Oscar Hammerstein II, book by Howard Lindsay and Russel Crouse, suggested by the true story,* The Trapp Family Singers, *by Maria Augusta Trapp. First produced: New York, 1959; London, 1961. Set in Austria in 1938.* (Performing rights: Williamson Music Limited.)

The postulant Maria is not ideally suited to the religious life, as the Mother Abbess of Nonnberg Abbey recognizes. Regretfully, she sends her out into the world as governess to the seven children of a retired Austrian Naval officer, Captain Georg von Trapp.

Since his wife's death Captain Trapp has managed his children through almost Naval discipline, and Maria finds them lacking warmth and response. It is only with singing lessons that she is able to break down their reserve, to find in the process that their musical talents are out of the ordinary. By the time the Captain has returned from an absence in Vienna the children have learned to sing in concert, so his bringing back with him an impresario, Max Detweiler, is a fortunate coincidence.

However, the Captain has also brought his fiancée, Elsa. Maria, sensing that she herself is falling in love with him, returns to the Abbey, only to be told by the Abbess that she must climb every mountain and face up to life, not run away from it. She returns to the Trapp villa to find that the Captain and Elsa are breaking their engagement, since their views about the rise of the Nazi Party differ sharply. The Captain soon realizes that he shares Maria's love, and they are married in the Abbey.

The Nazis take over Austria and order Captain von Trapp back to service at once. But Max Detweiler has arranged for the children to sing at the Karlsburg Festival, so Maria is able to delay her husband's departure by pointing out that his presence is needed at the important concert. He is allowed to be there, and at the end of the performance Max enables the entire family and Maria to escape to freedom by way of Nonnberg Abbey.

PRINCIPAL NUMBERS

Act 1 'Preludium' (Nuns)
    'The sound of music' (Maria)
    'Maria' (Sisters Berthe, Sophia, Margaretta and Abbess)
    'My favourite things' (Maria and Abbess)
    'Do-re-mi' (Maria and children)
    'Sixteen, going on seventeen' (Liesl and Rolf)
    'The lonely goatherd' (Maria and children)
    'How can love survive?' (Elsa, Max, Captain)
    'So long, farewell' (Children)
    'Climb ev'ry mountain' (Abbess)
Act 2 'No way to stop it' (Elsa, Max and Captain)
    'An ordinary couple' (Maria and Captain)
    'Edelweiss' (Captain, Maria and children)

South Pacific, *a musical in two acts. Music by Richard Rodgers, lyrics by Oscar Hammerstein II, book by Oscar Hammerstein II and Joshua Logan, based on James A. Michener's* Tales of the South Pacific. *First produced: New York, 1949; London, 1951. Set in the Pacific islands during the Second World War.* (Performing rights: Williamson Music Limited.)

Emile de Becque, a French planter, now middle-aged, has been living on a small Pacific island for some years, and has fathered two children there by a Polynesian woman, now dead. American warships are using the island as a base for operations against Japanese-held islands in the area, and Emile entertains to dinner a young and lovely Naval nurse, Ensign Nellie Forbush. He quickly falls in love with her, and although she has reservations about the difference between their ages his gentleness and charm captivate her. It is only when she learns about his relationship with a native woman that she finally cannot bear the thought of the marriage he is pressing upon her.

Emile is under pressure of another kind. A Lieutenant Cable wants him to put his knowledge of the islands at the Americans' disposal and guide them in a mission which could lead to an important victory over the Japanese. Having found impending happiness with Nellie, Emile has refused to risk his life; but when she rejects him he decides he has nothing more to hold him back and agrees to Cable's request. The mission is a huge success, though Cable is killed. Emile returns sadly to his home – to find Nellie awaiting him and playing with his children.

The chief sub-plot is about the attempts of an exotic woman of Chinese extraction, 'Bloody Mary', to marry

Cable off to her seventeen-year-old daughter Liat, on the neighbouring island of Bali Ha'i.

PRINCIPAL NUMBERS

Act 1 'Dites-moi'(Ngana and Jerome)
      'A cock-eyed optimist' (Nellie)
      'Some enchanted evening' (Emile)
      'Bloody Mary' (Sailors, Seabees and Marines)
      'There is nothin' like a dame' (Seabees)
      'Bali Ha'i' (Bloody Mary, Billis and Cable)
      'I'm gonna wash that man right out of my hair'
        (Nellie and Nurses)
      'A wonderful guy' (Nellie and Nurses)
      'Younger than springtime' (Cable)
      'This is how it feels' (Nellie and Emile)
Act 2 'Happy talk' (Bloody Mary)
      'Honey Bun' (Nellie, Billis and ensemble)
      'You've got to be carefully taught' (Cable)
      'This nearly was mine' (Emile)

The Street Singer, *a musical play in three acts. Music by Harold Fraser-Simson, book by Frederick Lonsdale, lyrics by Percy Greenbank with additional numbers by Ivy St Helier. First produced: London, 1924. Set in Paris early in the 19th century.* (Performing rights: Samuel French Ltd.)

The young Duchess of Versailles overhears in the artists' quarter of Paris a young artist, Bonni, imploring a dealer, Levy, to buy his picture, the last hope which could save him from penury. Levy adamantly refuses, telling him that some experience of starvation might make him a better artist. Fellow artists, models and friends gather at Bonni's studio to wish him farewell. A song is heard from outside and a poor little singing-girl is admitted. She says her name is Yvette. On the quiet, she persuades Levy to buy the picture and tell Bonni that a grand lady has taken a fancy to it.

Having changed Bonni's luck, Yvette is adopted as his mascot, and he paints her as 'The Street Singer' while she wears a dress bought for her by his grateful friends from Violette, a dressmaker in love with François, Bonni's misogynistic manservant. Violette breaks down François's defences, which occasions more revels.

During the revels a message is delivered summoning Bonni at once to the Duchess of Versailles, who wishes to inspect his new picture. To test out his affection for her, Yvette begs him not to go, but the opportunity to make another good sale is not to be missed. When he arrives at the Duchess's residence, he discovers that that lady is his own Yvette, who forgives him for putting his career before his love, but ensures that neither shall have precedence in future by making him ask her to marry him, and promptly accepting.

PRINCIPAL NUMBERS

Act 1 'Take life as it comes' (Bonni and chorus)
'Heart's desire' (Yvette)
'Fortune has smiled' (Yvette, Bonni and Levy)
'Follow Yvette' (Yvette)
Act 2 '*Père Patipou*' (Bonni and chorus)
'That's the sort of man' (Estelle and chorus)
''ow I 'ate women' (François)
'Just to hold you in my arms' (Bonni and Yvette)
'Husband No. 2' (François and Violette)
Act 3 'Too late' (Bonni and Yvette)
'That's what you are to me' (François and Violette)

The Student Prince, *a light opera in four acts. Music by Sigmund Romberg, book and lyrics by Dorothy Donnelly, based on the play,* Old Heidelberg, *by R. Bleichmann. First produced: New York, 1924; London, 1926. Set in 'Karlsberg' and Heidelberg in 1860.* (Performing rights: Pladio Limited.)

The heir to the throne of the fictional European kingdom of Karlsberg, Prince Karl, finds life at his father's Court formal and empty, and longs to recapture the pleasure of his days as a student in the old German university town of Heidelberg. His tutor, Dr Engel, also recalls 'golden days' spent there, and the two decide to pay a return visit.

Karl, arriving incognito as a former student, finds Heidelberg as entrancing as he had remembered it and gets a warm welcome from the new generation of students. They march boisterously to their favourite haunt, the Golden Apple Inn, where they sing rousing choruses and call for the landlord's daughter, Kathie, to sing for them, which she does with a will. Karl is attracted to her at once, and their attachment soon ripens into mutual love, although Karl knows that he is destined to marry Princess Margaret of his own State, who, meanwhile, is enjoying herself back in Karlsberg with a gallant Captain Tarnitz.

Word reaches Karl that the King is dead and that he must return to assume the throne. He obeys, but is soon yearning for Heidelberg and Kathie. Doomed to disappointment, he goes back there and finds the whole atmosphere changed, now that he is known to be a King and no longer the students' equal. It is also obvious to them both that he and Kathie can never become anything more to one another than lovers in spirit, and they part wistfully, to subsist on their memories.

Prologue 'Golden Days' (Karl and Engel)
Act 1 'To the inn we're marching' (Students and Kathie)
'Drinking Song' (Students)
'*Gaudeamus*' (Students)
'Deep in my heart, dear' (Kathie and Karl)
'Serenade' (Karl)
Act 2 'Student life' (Chorus)
'Thoughts will come back to me' (Karl)
Act 3 'Just we two' (Princess and Tarnitz)
Act 4 'Let us sing a song' (Students)

The Three Musketeers, *a romantic musical play in three acts. Music by Rudolf Friml, book by Anthony McGuire based on Alexandre Dumas's novel, lyrics by Clifford Grey. First produced: New York, 1928; London, 1930. Set in Paris and London in the early 17th century.* (Performing rights: Chappell & Co. Ltd.)

The Three Musketeers of King Louis XIII's bodyguard – Athos, Porthos and Aramis – are enjoying an habitual carousal at the Jolly Miller Inn, where they are joined by the penniless Gascon, D'Artagnan, who arrives on his emaciated white horse. His natural resource is soon to be put to the test. The Queen (Anne) is at the height of her passionate *affaire* with England's Duke of Buckingham and has recently given him as a token of love a diamond heart, a present from the King to her. The trouble-making Cardinal Richelieu has heard about this and has persuaded the King to insist on the Queen wearing the jewel at a forthcoming gala. Meanwhile, Richelieu has dispatched the Comte de Rochefort and Lady de Winter – known as 'Milady' – to London to get back the jewel by any means and return it to Richelieu, who plans to produce it at the gala and thus reveal to Louis his Queen's treachery.

At the same time the Queen has sent her confidential lady-in-waiting, Constance, to entreat the Musketeers to recover the jewel in time for her to wear it and confound her enemies. They hasten to London, to find that 'Milady' has already gained possession of it. D'Artagnan promptly lays seige to her as a lover, and, embracing her closely manages to snatch the jewel from her bosom. De Rochefort enters and the two men fight a hectic duel with swords, on and around 'Milady's' bed, at the end of which de Rochefort is slain. The Musketeers get back to France in time to hand over the jewel for the Queen to produce it at Louis' demand and sweetly assure him that she had only been waiting for him to fasten it to her shoulder with his own hands, in the way he had originally done.

PRINCIPAL NUMBERS

Act 1 'We're all for one' (Athos, Porthos and Aramis)
'Heart of mine' (Constance and D'Artagnan)
'My sword and I' (D'Artagnan and chorus)
'My dreams' (Queen)
'Love is the sun' (Queen, Buckingham and Constance)
'Your eyes' (Constance and D'Artagnan)
Act 2 '*Ma belle*' (Aramis and chorus)
'One kiss' (Constance and D'Artagnan)
Pages' Dance
'Queen of my heart' (Buckingham)
'Ev'ry little while' (Constance)

Tom Jones, *a comic opera in three acts based on the novel by Henry Fielding. Music by Edward German, book by Alexander M. Thompson and Robert Courtneidge, lyrics by Charles H. Taylor. First produced: Manchester, 1907; London, 1907. Set in Somerset and London in the mid-18th century.* (Performing rights: Chappell & Co. Ltd.)

Tom Jones, an orphan of unknown birth, has been adopted by a Somersetshire magistrate, Squire Allworthy, whose rich nephew Blifil is engaged to marry Sophia, the only child of a neighbour, Squire Western. But Tom and Sophia are in love. When Blifil discovers Tom comforting Sophia, who has just heard that her father has signed the marriage contract between her and Blifil, he insults Tom, who knocks him down, with the consequence that Allworthy renounces him.

Tom and Sophia leave their homes, though not together. Squire Western and Blifil pursue Sophia and her maid Honour and chance to put up at the very inn where the two women and Tom Jones are spending the night, unaware that they are under the same roof. Also at the inn is Sophia's worldly friend Lady Bellaston, who had been attacked by a highwayman and rescued by Tom Jones, to whom she has become so attracted that she gives it out that they are husband and wife. Benjamin Partridge, the village barber who has been summoned to try to alleviate an attack of gout Squire Western is suffering, hears the name Tom Jones, and mentions that he is at the inn. Tom and Lady Bellaston are found in her room. When word of this reaches Sophia she leaves, after writing a note telling Tom she wants nothing more to do with him. Determining to join the army, he accepts Lady Bellaston's offer of a lift to London in her coach.

Partridge had known the truth about Tom's birth – he turns out to be Blifil's brother – and has conveyed it to Squire Western. The Squire hastens to London to consent to a marriage between Sophia and Tom, who is far from being the penniless foundling he had been supposed. He is able to explain the innocence of his relationship with Lady Bellaston, who is Sophia's sponsor in London society, and the young lovers are reunited.

PRINCIPAL NUMBERS

Act 1 'On a January morning' (Western and chorus)
'West Country lad' (Tom and chorus)
'The Barley Mow' (Ensemble)
'Here's a paradise for lovers' (Sophia, Honour, Tom and Allworthy)
'For aye, my love' (Tom)

Act 2 'A person of parts' (Partridge and chorus)
'Dream o' day Jill' (Sophia)
Laughing trio: 'You have a pretty wit' (Honour, Gregory, and Partridge)
'A soldier's scarlet coat' (Tom and chorus)

Act 3 Morris dance and Gavotte: 'Glass of fashion' (Ensemble)
'The green ribbon' (Honour and male chorus)
'If love's content' (Tom)
Waltz song: 'For tonight, for tonight' (Sophia)

The Toreador, *a musical play in two acts. Music by Ivan Caryll and Lionel Monckton, book by James T. Tanner and Harry Nicholls, lyrics by Adrian Ross and Percy Greenbank. First produced: London, 1901. Set in Biarritz and Villaya, Spain, in contemporary period.* (Performing rights: Chappell & Co. Ltd.)

A marriage is impending between a rich widow, Mrs Malton Hoppings, and a celebrated toreador, Carajola. This is complicated by the fact that he is engaged to a girl named Teresa, and that Mrs Hoppings is closely followed by her admirer, Pettifer, a dealer in wild animals. He is to supply the bulls for Carajola's next fight, only it is arranged that instead of bulls a tiger will enter the arena with Carajola. Pettifer advertises for one. The advertisement is answered by Sammy Gigg, a human 'tiger', as footmen who rode on their employers' carriages used to be known.

Further elements of the highly complex 'story' include a Carlist plot in Spain, which Carajola is expected to lead, and a 'Mr and Mrs Robinson', who are, respectively, Nancy Staunton, wearing male clothes, and her friend Dora Selby, a Ward in Chancery – a deception designed to get rid of Dora's hordes of unwanted male admirers, prominent among whom is her guardian's nephew, Augustus Traill. Nancy has her own pursuer, Sir Archibald Slackitt, Bart, a not-very-bright lieutenant of the Welsh Guards.

After numerous entanglements, including the mistaking of the animal-dealer for the toreador himself, which almost results in his having to enter the bullring, Carajola finishes up with Teresa, Mrs Hoppings with Pettifer, and 'the Robinsons' with their respective suitors.

136

Act 1 'I've always had a passion' (Mrs Hoppings and chorus)
'Toreador Song' (Carajola and chorus)
'Captivating Cora' (Cora)
'Everybody's awfully good to me' (Archibald)
'If ever I marry' (Susan and Gigg)
'My Zoo' (Pettifer and chorus)
'Husband and wife' (Dora and Nancy)
'España' (Dora, Nancy, Augustus and Archibald)
'The language of the flowers' (Nancy)
Act 2 'The Governor of Villaya' (Governor and chorus)
'When I marry Amelia' (Pettifer)
'My Toreador' (La Belle Bolero)
'Punch and Judy' (Susan and Gigg)
'Archie' (Archibald and chorus)

The Vagabond King, *a musical play in four acts. Music by Rudolf Friml, book and lyrics by Brian Hooker and W. H. Post, based on Justin Huntly McCarthy's romance,* If I Were King. *First produced: New York, 1925; London, 1927. Set in Paris in the 15th century.* (Performing rights: Samuel French Ltd.)

François Villon, drunken criminal, romantic poet and acknowledged King of the Vagabonds of Paris, has been sending poems to the high-born Katherine de Vaucelles, who is unaware of his identity but intrigued by the passion of his sentiments. She has rejected the advances of the universally disliked King Louis XI, who is looking for an opportunity to humble her, at a time when he would be better concerning himself with the armies of Burgundian rebels already surrounding the city.

Attending the vagabonds' revels in disguise, the King sees Villon, just out of gaol, with the mistress he no longer cares for, Huguette du Hamel, who always wears male attire, and his friend Guy Taberie. Villon boasts to the mob what he would do if he were king for a day. Louis, seeing his chance, has him summoned to Court and offers him twenty-four hours' rule as Grand Marshal. In this time he must win Katherine and lead the vagabonds to successful victory over the Burgundians, or he will be hanged.

Villon cleans himself up and dresses as befits his temporary high office. The vagabonds manage to defeat the Burgundians, but Villon uncovers a plot to assassinate the King. He swaps clothes with Louis, attracting the would-be murderer to himself. It is Huguette who saves his life at the cost of her own, and dies in his arms. Villon has conquered Katherine with his verse, but this is not enough to fulfil the ungrateful King's stipulations and he decrees that Villon must die. Katherine saves him by claiming him as her husband, under an old feudal law. The King concurs, satisfied that the life she will face with the Vagabond King will amply repay her for daring to rebuff a real monarch.

PRINCIPAL NUMBERS

Act 1   'Love for sale' (Huguette and chorus)
  'What care I for a purse of gold' (Taberie and men)
  'Song of the vagabonds' (Villon and chorus)
  'Some day' (Katherine)
  'Only a rose' (Katherine and Villon)

138

Act 2 'Hunting' (Noel and ensemble)
      'Tomorrow' (Katherine and Villon)
Act 3 'Nocturne' (Ensemble)
      Ballet: Tarantella
      'Lullaby' (Taberie, Oliver, Lady Mary)
      'Love me tonight' (Katherine and Villon)
Act 4 Church music
      Victory March

Discography

As with *The Vintage Operetta Book*, I am indebted for this discography to Mr Frank Rogers, of The Gramophone Exchange Limited, 80–82 Wardour Street, London WIV 4BD (telephone 01-427 5313), to whom I would refer any inquirers after these or other recordings in these fields. Again, no record numbers or details of labels are shown, principally because recordings are often reissued by different companies from the originating ones, using their own labelling and numbering, which can lead to confusion. Mention of the title and principal artists is enough for a record dealer to go by.

Except where indicated these recordings are all sung in English; and all offer fairly substantial selections from the respective shows. A mass of recordings exists of individual numbers, but there is no space to include them here, and they can easily be traced through the gramophone catalogues by reference to the title of the show. Neither have I given details of long-deleted recordings, which can only be pursued through specialist dealers. I have, however, admitted works belonging to the period under review which have not been dealt with in the body of the book.

AFTER THE BALL, Coward: Ellis, Lee, Graves. *Cond.* Martell

ALADDIN, Porter: Richard, King, Alberghetti
Monkhouse, Morron, Shiner. *Cond.* Howell
ALL AMERICAN, Strouse: Bolger, Herlie
ANNIE GET YOUR GUN, Berlin: Merman, Yarnell, Venuta. *Cond.* Allers
Martin, Raitt
Bruhl, Trehy (in German)
Hutton, Keel
Day, Goulet
ANYA, Wright and Forrest: Towers, Kermoyan, Gish
APPLAUSE, Strouse: Bacall, Cariou, Mandan
ARCADIANS, THE, Monckton and Talbot: Bronhill, Howard, Cole. *Cond.* Tausky
Glover, Minty, Bowman. *Cond.* Vinter
BABES IN ARMS, Rodgers: Martin
BABES IN TOYLAND, Herbert: Baker, Kemble (coupled with *Red Mill, The (q.v.)*)
BITTER SWEET, Coward: Leigh, Pease, Hampshire. *Cond.* Alwyn
Bronhill, Jason. *Cond.* Douglas
Dawn, Lee, Cardinale
BLESS THE BRIDE, Ellis: Millar, Cardinale, Mount. *Cond.* Love
BOYS FROM SYRACUSE, THE, Rodgers: Monkhouse, Quilley, Fitzgibbon
Cassidy, Nelson, Osterwald
Hanley, Damon, Marie
BRIGADOON, Loewe: Jones, Cassiday, Johnson, Porretta. *Cond.* Engel
Peerce, Merrill, Powell
BY JUPITER, Rodgers: Bolger, Moore, Venuta
CABIN IN THE SKY, Duke: Le Noire, Lester, Middleton. *Cond.* Oliver

CALL ME MADAM, Berlin: Worth, Walbrook, Wallis. *Cond*. Ornadell

Shore, Lukas, Nype

Merman, Haymes

CAN CAN, Porter: Lilo, Cookson, Conried. *Cond*. Rosenstock

Hilda, Hockridge

CARELESS RAPTURE, Novello: Ellis, Jones, Dickson

CAROUSEL, Rodgers: Raitt, Christy, Watson, Horton
Macrae, Jones, Mitchell

Goulet, Grover, Roberts, Neway

CAT AND THE FIDDLE, THE, Kern: Hume, Quilley

CHU CHIN CHOW, Norton: Alan, Grimaldi, Lawrence. *Cond*. Hollingsworth

Te Wiata, Byran, Leigh. *Cond*. Collins

CINDERELLA, Rodgers: Martin, Sanders. *Cond*. Scherman
Rogers, Pidgeon, Holm

CONVERSATION PIECE, Coward: Pons, Coward, Nesbitt, Burton. *Cond*. Engel

DANCING YEARS, THE, Novello: Howard, Cole, Kennedy
Bronhill, Knight, Giacomini

Beaumont, Ellis, Gilbert

DEEP IN MY HEART, Romberg: Traubel, Keel, Martin. *Cond*. Deutsch

DESERT SONG, THE, Romberg: Macrae, Kirsten. *Cond*. Alexander

Hockridge, Bronhill. *Cond*. Collins

Barr, Tozzi, Palmer. *Cond*. Engel

EILEEN, Herbert: Al Goodman Orchestra and Soloists

FINIAN'S RAINBOW, Lane: Logan, Richards, Wayne. *Cond*. Charles

FIREFLY, THE, Friml: Paul Britten Orchestra (coupled with *Naughty Marietta* (*q.v.*))

142

FLOWER DRUM SONG, Rodgers: Blyden, Hall, Kenney, Umeki

FUNNY FACE, Gershwin: Astaire, Hepburn

GEISHA, THE, Jones: Falvay, Dekner, Seegers, Muench. *Cond.* Dobrindt (in German)

GIRL CRAZY, Gershwin: Martin, Carlyle, Chappell

GIRL IN PINK TIGHTS, THE, Romberg: Jeanmaire

GIRL WHO CAME TO SUPPER, THE, Coward: Ferrer, Henderson

GLAMOROUS NIGHT, Novello: Woodland, Sinclair, Thomas. *Cond.* Dods

Ellis, Jones, Dickson

GUYS AND DOLLS, Loesser: Blaine, Levene, Alda, Bigley

HELLO, DOLLY, Herman: Martini, Petry, Kollo, Millowitsch

HIT THE DECK, Youmans: Martin, Powell, Reynolds

Hume, Quilley

JUMBO, Rodgers: Day, Raye, Durante

KEAN, Wright and Forrest: Venora, Gray, Weldon

KING'S RHAPSODY, Novello: Lee, Gilbert, Dare

Glover, Kern, Westbury. *Cond.* Tausky

KING AND I, THE, Rodgers: Matthews, Lucas, Peters. *Cond.* Love

Hobson, Lom, Duke

Stevens, McGavin, Venora, Porreta

Kerr, Brynner, Moreno

KISMET, Wright and Forrest: Jeffreys, Venora, Drake

McKellar, Merrill, Resnik

KISS ME KATE, Porter: Hilda, Hockridge

Drake, Morison, Kirk

Moorefields, Alexander (in German)

LEAVE IT TO JANE, Kern: Murray, Greener, Mango

LADY BE GOOD, Gershwin: Astaire, Astaire

MAID OF THE MOUNTAINS, THE, Fraser-Simson: Stevens, Wakeham, Williams. *Cond.* Farrow

Collins, Bates, de Frece, Lester, Sealby

MERRIE ENGLAND, German: McAlpine, Bronhill, Glossop. *Cond.* Collins

MISS LIBERTY, Berlin: Albert, McLerie, McCarty, Dingle

MR PRESIDENT, Berlin: Ryan, Fabray, Gillette

MOST HAPPY FELLA, THE, Loesser: Weede, Sullivan, Lund. *Cond.* Greene

Te Wiata, Scott, Lund

Steffe, Grimaldi

MUSIC IN THE AIR, Kern: Grimaldi, Cole

Pickens

MY FAIR LADY, Loewe: Alexander, Konya, Kraner (in German)

Andrews, Harrison, Holloway

NEW MOON, THE, Romberg: Macrae, Kirsten, Robinson

NAUGHTY MARIETTA, Herbert: Paul Britten Orchestra (coupled with *Firefly, The* (*q.v.*))

Macrae, Piazza (coupled with *Red Mill, The* (*q.v.*))

NO, NO, NANETTE, Youmans: Martin, Adams

Burton, Preston, Parker

Grossmith, Hale, Pearce

Keeler, Gilford, Van, Kelly

Fontagnère, Duvaleix, Rogers, Dachary, Berton (in (French; coupled with *Rose Marie* (*q.v.*))

OF THEE I SING, Gershwin: Carson, Hartman

OH KAY, Gershwin: Ruick, Cassidy, Case, White. *Cond.* Engel

Daniels, Stevens

OKLAHOMA!, Rogers: Drake, Roberts, Holm

Eddy, Haskins

Raitt, Henderson

Hagara, Kauffeld, Kuhn (in German)

(Film Version) Macrae, Jones

ON THE TOWN, Bernstein: Gould, McKay, Kiser

ON YOUR TOES, Rodgers: Van, Coulter, Stritch

Nelson, Cassidy

PAJAMA GAME, THE, Adler and Ross: Raitt, E. Foy jnr,
Paige

(Film Version) Doris Day

PAL JOEY, Rodgers: Segal, Lang

Froman, Beavers

PERCHANCE TO DREAM, Novello: Howard, Robson,
Bowman. *Cond*. Dods

Barron, Gilbert, Beaumont

PINS AND NEEDLES, Rome: Carroll, Streisand, Bretton

RED MILL, THE, Herbert: Wrightson, Briney, Dame
Evans, Farrell

Farrell, Evans, Knight (coupled with *Babes in Toyland* (*q.v.*))

Macrae (coupled with *Naughty Marietta* (*q.v.*))

ROBERTA, Kern: Carlisle, Drake, Laurence

Grimaldi, Cole, Fitzgibbon

Cassidy, Roberts, Ballard

ROSE MARIE, Friml: Hughes, Leigh, Cole

Andrews, Tozzi, Day, Tzelniker

Fontagnère, Rogers, Duvaleix, Dachary (in French;
coupled with *No, No, Nanette* (*q.v.*))

Keel, Blyth, Lamas

SALAD DAYS, Slade: Drew, Warner

SHOWBOAT, Kern: Lawrence, Lucas, Scott, Moray

Jobin, Lane, Carey, Nelson

Clayton, Bruce, Spencer

Raitt, Cook, Warfield

Bronhill, Williams, Dawn

Kelly, Gardner, Keel

SONG OF NORWAY, Wright: Brooks, Bliss, Shafer, Arno
  Lewis, Reardon, Scott, Olvis
  Elliott, Hughes, Round, Lawrenson
SOUND OF MUSIC, Rodgers: Bikel, Martin, Neway
  Schirrmacher, Felgen (in German)
SOUTH PACIFIC, Rodgers: Gaynor, Kerr, Brazzi, Hall
STUDENT PRINCE, THE, Romberg: Melchior, Wilson
    (coupled with *Vagabond King, The* (*q.v.*))
  Kirsten, Rounseville. *Cond.* Engel
  Peters, Peerce, Tozzi
  Macrae, Warenskjuld
SUNNY, Kern: Hulbert, Hale, Buchanan, Randolph
SWEETHEARTS, Herbert: Al Goodman Orchestra and
  Soloists
UP IN CENTRAL PARK, Romberg: Evans, Farrell, Holm
VAGABOND KING, THE, Friml: Kirkop, Grayson,
  Moreno
  Staffe, Larson
  Drake, Benzell, Bible (coupled with *Student Prince,
    The* (*q.v.*))
  Lanza, Raskin
WATER GIPSIES, THE, Ellis: Bryan, Charles, Payne
WEDDING IN PARIS, May: Walbrook, Layne, Warren
WEST SIDE STORY, Bernstein: Thomas, Phillips